STILL THE HAPPIEST PEOPLE

RICHARD SHAKARIAN

STILL THE HAPPIEST PEOPLE
Copyright © 2012, by Richard Shakarian

All rights reserved. No part of this publication may be reproduced, stored in a retrieval system, or transmitted in any form by means electronic, mechanical, photocopying, recording or otherwise, except for the inclusion of brief quotations in a review, without prior permission in writing from the publisher.

ISBN: 978-0-9846515-4-2

Published by

LIFEBRIDGE
BOOKS
P.O. Box 49428
Charlotte, NC 28277
www.LifeBridgeBooks.com

Printed in the United States of America

Love is Forever

DEDICATION

To my dear wife, Vangie. Since the day we met as sweethearts in college, she has been the light of my life. Even in the most challenging moments, her encouragement and faith has carried us to a better day. Traveling the world together, Vangie is a role model for tens of thousands of the Ladies of the Fellowship. She is known for her grace and beauty. Her example and influence has helped many.

To my dad, Demos. He was my closest friend. Even when he was hurting, his gentle spirit reached out with love to help others. We worked together almost every day from my college years until the Lord called him home. We shared his inspiration and vision which filled our lives, and it still lives today in the hearts of millions of people.

To my beloved grandfather, Isaac. As the head of an immigrant family at the age of 15, he was the sole support for his mother and five sisters. With wisdom, hard work, and a prophetic promise, he established the family business. He helped shape the formative years of my life. From him I learned the old world ways and strategic thinking which enabled me to speak to prominent and powerful men around the world.

To our beautiful children and grandchildren, who are continuing the Shakarian family legacy.

Special appreciation to our extended family, the hundreds of thousands of members and friends of the Fellowship. And to the thousands of volunteers as you carry the torch and transform nations.

Contents

Chapter 1	The Fire!	11
Chapter 2	Escape from Kara Kala	31
Chapter 3	Cows, Cows, and More Cows!	45
Chapter 4	Much More Than Business	63
Chapter 5	Eighty Amazing Days	87
Chapter 6	The Master's Plan	101
Chapter 7	A Hunger for Freedom	123
Chapter 8	A New Day	135
Chapter 9	The Confirmation	145
Chapter 10	Opening Palace Doors	155
Chapter 11	Flags of Faith	181
Chapter 12	Truly, a Better Life	193

Introduction

I am thrilled you are reading this book. It tells the dramatic birth and growth of what we call "the Fellowship" —a powerful movement that has been "flying under the radar," yet is transforming the lives of millions around the globe.

Every week, in Europe, Africa, Asia, and the Americas, there are thousands of meetings where business men and women share their personal stories of how they have found new hope and a better life.

As one historian observed, "You may not readily find the statistics of this organization, but it is having a profound effect in nation after nation."

For example, you will learn that in one Central American country, more than half of its 6 million citizens have been personally prayed with by members and volunteers of our organization.

This is not an ordinary journey. It begins in Armenia, where the prophecy of an 11-year-old boy resulted in our family escaping the Armenian genocide and moving to Los Angeles. There, my grandfather, Isaac, started a business that became the largest dairy in the United States.

You'll also learn how his son—my father—Demos

Shakarian, had a vision that would have a spiritual impact on the world. This has happened—and I am honored to be leading this movement in the 21st century.

On these pages I want to share behind-the-scene stories:

- Pioneering a new marketing concept of "Drive in Dairies."
- How I met the love of my life, Vangie.
- The miracles that occurred during an "Around the World in 80 Days" journey.
- Conducting some of the largest youth rallies ever held in the United States.
- Adventures in oil exploration and real estate.
- A series of prophecies that shaped my future.
- The vision of the Seven Great Pillars.
- What took place during meetings with world leaders, including Ariel Sharon in Israel, Mobuto in the Congo, and Daniel Ortgega in Nicaragua.
- The amazing work of "Fire Teams."
- The God-given plan that has revolutionized the Fellowship and is touching the lives of millions.

Over the years, I have been asked many times, "Richard, why do you believe your family was spared when so many others suffered because of the massacre in Armenia?"

The answer is detailed in this book. It is evident when we see what is taking place through the Fellowship—a movement led by thousands of dedicated men and women who are united as one, regardless of culture, politics, religion, language, or location.

This grass roots effort is the result of a divine mandate that we break the chains of despair by taking the message of God's love to every family, in every nation.

I believe you will be inspired and challenged by what you are about to read.

– Richard Shakarian

Chapter 1

The Fire!

I was settled in my hotel room in Managua, Nicaragua, looking out the window at the brilliant red skies and dark clouds as the sun was setting. It had been an extremely humid, busy day in early May, 1999—following one of the most exhilarating weeks of my life. I was exhausted!

Suddenly the phone rang and I was diverted from my thoughts. "Richard," said a voice on the line, "Daniel Ortega would like you to come to his compound tonight. He wants to meet you."

It didn't take me long to figure out why! Every day for the previous week I had been followed by television cameras and news reporters. Our organization was making headlines because of the impact we were having on thousands upon thousands of people in this war-weary country.

Obviously, Ortega had seen the video of my meeting with the then-Nicaraguan, president, Arnoldo Aleman, and he wanted to know what was going on.

I learned that Ortega, the son of a shoemaker was still a teenager when he joined the Sandinistas. In 1967 he was imprisoned for robbing a bank to raise funds for the revolution. After spending seven years in jail, being severely tortured, he was released along with other prisoners in exchange for hostages.

In 1979, following a bitter armed struggle, President Somoza fled into exile and the Sandinistas took the reigns of power, inheriting a country in ruins.

Ortega became a member of a five person Junta of National Reconciliation, and in 1984 was elected president for the next six years.

Even though he was now out of power, his party still carried tremendous political clout in the government and among the people.

Ground Zero

Not knowing what was ahead for us, about 15 of our national leaders, plus my wife, Vangie, headed for the compound. On the way, I turned to Vangie and admitted, "I really don't have anything special to say to him. I wish I did." To be honest, there were butterflies churning in my stomach anticipating the impending encounter.

Our caravan arrived at what looked like an old Western fort you would expect to see in the movies. Above us was an imposing machine gun tower and armed guards were protecting a 15-foot wooden front gate. This was ground zero for the FSLN, *Frente Sandinista de Liberación Nacional*—the Sandinista National Liberation Front.

Patiently, we waited at the entrance to the fortress while the tough-looking security men checked us out. Soon, one of the soldiers called out my name: "Richard!" he said.

"That's me," I answered.

The gate swung open and our group drove onto the grounds. We were soon ushered into a building which was decorated with photos of martyred Marxist-Leninist Sandinistas.

I drew a deep breath as we were led into a room which held about 30 people. It was the very room where Ortega and his men strategized war moves against the United States, who at one time supported the Contras—a right wing militia. During the ten-year violent armed struggle that began in 1980, over 50,000 lives were lost and 150,000 Nicaraguans fled into exile.

Down the hall were steps leading to a bomb shelter.

Fifteen of Ortega's top generals were already congregated there, and when we arrived the room was jammed to capacity.

Daniel walked in wearing a smartly-tailored khaki outfit. At the time his title was "Comandante" and you could sense his aura as a leader. He looks people straight in the eyes and you know immediately who is in charge.

We took our seats at the front of the room behind a long table. His chair was next to mine, but because the room was so crowded our shoulders and arms were touching.

Protocol is for the host to speak first, but as he began his official welcome, I looked at the back of the room and saw camera men from our team who were from Honduras. They were standing by an open door shooting video. Quickly, I politely interrupted, signaled for the photographers to stop and said, "Comandante, we are not here to take advantage of anything. These men are filming, and if you will allow them to continue, this footage will be seen around the world. If not, they will put the cameras down. What is your wish?"

Ortega had no problem with us filming and we have a record of the meeting.

As part of his opening remarks, he talked about the oppression of the Nicaraguan people and expressed that he felt justified in "doing whatever we have to do" to alleviate the "unjust suffering" under the current system of government. He spoke at length of the excesses and inconsistencies of the present administration and bragged how the Sandinistas were better armed than the national troops, adding, "It's in our hands to take control once more."

Something Stirring Deep Inside

After his remarks, I responded briefly, then several others spoke. Sitting around that table were military leaders who had been involved in some of the most brutal acts of war imaginable. Also present were men on our team who had been victims of the Sandinistas years earlier. One man was with us whose father-in-law owned a huge dairy business. When Ortega was president, they confiscated the farm and all the cows. The rationale being that this was for the good of the people so he should be happy to forfeit his land. The mother of another man had been thrown into prison, accused of being a spy until it was proved otherwise.

Yet this evening, not one person mentioned the past. No

one was aggrieved. There was no bitterness expressed as we sat there together.

As various people from our team were briefly sharing their stories of how their lives had been changed by Christ, all of a sudden I felt something stirring deep inside that I needed to say—but wasn't sure whether I should or not. Why? Because I didn't know if it was appropriate knowing Ortega's turbulent history. I didn't want him to feel I was endorsing his political and miliary movement.

However, the Lord kept speaking to my spirit, letting me know that I was just a conduit and must not keep what I had to say to myself. So I turned and said, "Comandante, I have a word from the Lord for you."

A hush fell across that crowded room as Ortega slowly turned to look at me. Such words had never been spoken on that compound before. The atmosphere seemed charged with electricity—and everybody felt it. Goosebumps were sitting on goosebumps!

"GOD SAID..."

Before I could open my mouth to speak, a strong-minded, Marxist general headed straight for the door, attempting to leave. One of our Honduran camera men, sensing he was upset, placed his hand on the man's back and said, "Don't go. Settle down. Everything is alright."

Suddenly, the general exclaimed, "The heat! The heat! It's burning me!"

"What heat?"

He told the camera man, "Your hand is burning my back." Without question, God's supernatural presence was everywhere.

I've never been in a situation like this before or since. It was as if a cloud of glory descended and a warm blanket of anointing dropped into the room.

The first words were extremely difficult for me to utter, but I began: "God said you are a great leader." Then I continued, "You are a great leader of men, but if you put forth your hand to correct that which is wrong, the nation will be broken. It will be worse for the people and worse for you personally than before. But if you ask God, He will show you the way."

Then I said, "Remember the time Moses was leading his people out of bondage and reached a place of impossibility where they were trapped. Moses cried out to God for help and the Lord made a path of escape for the children of Israel through the Red Sea." I explained, "The reason this was possible is because God is the one who makes the road."

At that point I looked around and saw several of the Sandinistas nodding in agreement. I added, "If you ask God to help your nation, it doesn't mean that He is going to answer the next day and feed all the people. But it does mean that it is His problem, not yours—and He will take over and find a way to heal the country. You won't be harmed, and everyone will be helped."

I also said, "No one in this room knows the way, I don't know it, nor do others, but God does. He will act according to His plan and the people will be blessed."

Then I turned once more to Ortega and asked, "Now I would like to pray for your nation. Would that be alright?"

He responded, "Yes,"

I reached out to take his hand and he gave me a strong grip. I prayed a short prayer, dedicating him and the people of Nicaragua to the Lord.

A Long Pause

When I had finished, everyone looked up at me except Ortega. He did not let go of my hand, holding it very tightly. I felt there was something happening in the heart of this man and I said, "Comandante, would you like to ask God to show you the way for your country?"

There was a long pause and we had no idea what was going to happen next.

Then, in Spanish, Daniel began a soft, short prayer. This is the translation: "Thank You, Lord, for this meeting that will serve to bring the nation closer to You. That it might come out of its pain, out of its crisis, so that it can be filled with hope, faith, and joy. Lord, thank You."

When he finished there was a wave of peace that washed over the room. Ortega opened his eyes and there was a big smile on his face—and a glow as if a heavy load had been lifted.

In my mind's eye I could see the painting by Michelangelo in Rome's Sistine Chapel where the finger of God reached down and touched the finger of man. I truly believe that night the Almighty touched Daniel Ortega.

He continued holding my hand, shaking it, telling me, "Thank you, thank you. You'll never know what this means to me."

After the meeting had concluded, one of his generals came to me and confided, "I've been with him for 25 years and this is the first time I have ever heard him pray."

An Amazing Mission

Before you get the impression that I am a preacher or an evangelist, that is not my calling. I am a businessman who loves God and heads an organization that is literally changing the spiritual tide of nation after nation around the world.

Later I will share how God raised up the FGBMFI—Full Gospel Business Men's Fellowship International—for a truly amazing mission. That's quite a mouthful, so in this book I'll just refer to it as the Fellowship.

This wasn't my first visit to Nicaragua. I had traveled to this land of lakes and volcanoes many times to meet with the leaders of our organization that had about 35 chapters in the late 1990s.

I earlier mentioned my meeting with president Arnoldo Aleman, who always welcomed me at the presidential palace every time I was in the country. In many nations, we are received by the head of state and discuss spiritual matters and the influence of business people to affect positive change.

One of those visits was in the fall of 1998, about six

months before the Ortega encounter I just detailed.

I was in Nicaragua to encourage our leaders to help bring healing to a people who had been ravaged by war and revolution. The Contra conflict cost over $150 billion and had practically destroyed the country's infrastructure—not to mention the emotional toll on its citizens.

One of the men who served coffee in the president's chamber was a member of the Fellowship and he always took excellent care of us during those meetings. At this particular time, however, even though my extended conversation with Aleman concerned faith, I left the palace with a heavy heart. I was deeply concerned about the future of Nicaragua.

A Mandate from Above

The next morning, when some of our men picked me up for the day's activities, I told them, "I'd really like to go over to Pope John Paul II Plaza and spend a little time in prayer." I let them know that something was disturbing me and I needed to pray about it.

When we reached the park, close to Lake Managua near the presidential offices, I walked a short distance away from those with me to be alone with my thoughts.

This location had experienced earthquakes, volcanoes, dictatorships, Marxism, and war. At one time, the Sandinistas cleared the park for hundreds of thousands to demonstrate.

As I walked through these historic grounds, my heart

was aching. I felt the burden of a people who had been so hurt by injustice and forces that seemed beyond their control.

For one hour I prayed, then suddenly I received what I can only describe as an "inspiration" and a "command" from above. Some would call it a "prophetic word."

In the next hour I received seven commands:

First: *Focus on Nicaragua. God has seen their sufferings and heard their prayers.*

Second: *Tell of His love and pray for one person in every family in the nation, from the home of the President to the farthest Indian village. That one person would be the seed for the family to be saved. Through the families, the nation would be redeemed.*

Third: *Tell our story of a better life in every city, every suburb, every town, every village, and at every crossroads. Let every family know of God's love and care for them.*

Fourth: *Begin the first week of May. This turned out to be a very important date. Labor and Marxist forces had teamed up to close down the nation. Only decisive action saved Nicaragua from civil war.*

Fifth, sixth, and seventh: *Beware of three dangers: political, ecological, and geological. (All three were in the news the day we began.)*

Nothing like this had ever happened to me before. I felt like Moses of old when he was at the burning bush and God instructed him, "Go and set My people free!"

At first, Moses objected because he didn't want the daunting task—plus he didn't know how to undertake such a monumental mission. Finally God told him, "Just go and do it!"

The Almighty asked Moses, "What is in your hand?" He didn't have anything of value. Just a stick—a simple rod.

I walked out of that park literally shaken by what I had just received. It was an overwhelming mandate, but I thought, "How can a few men reach 6 million people? How can we pray for one person in every family? That would be at least 2 million people!

The answer was clear. We were to start with what was in our hand, no matter how insignificant or small.

There was one more part to the mandate. God clearly impressed on me, "You are to begin this project in Nicaragua on May 4, 1999."

Wow! A divine plan with a specific timetable.

Would they Reject Me?

Already on the schedule was a meeting in Miami, Florida, with the regional and national directors of the Fellowship from Latin American countries.

As the January 1999 date drew closer, I became extremely concerned. How can I explain this to our leaders? These were successful business people who had been doing things in the Fellowship in certain ways for years. They operated with tried and true methods and patterns that were successful, but they were not reaching entire nations with the Good News.

This would be a new concept that was not part of our organizational culture or tradition. Yet, as I will share later, it was one which was included in the original vision given to my father, Demos Shakarian, when the Fellowship was founded in the 1950s.

Even though this was my own burning bush experience and I felt strongly about it, I kept thinking, "What if they reject the mandate God has given me?"

Many have experienced epiphanies—life-changing moments when something drops into their spirit. They know it is meant to be, but if they are the only person to receive it, how can others catch the same vision?

Just before the Miami conference, I had foot surgery so I was sitting on a stool in front of our Latin leaders. Our vice president, John Carrette, interpreted for me in Spanish.

"Men," I began," the subject this morning is 'How Does God See a Nation?'"

I turned their attention to the suffering of God's people in Egypt under the rule of Pharaoh. We talked about how God was so concerned over their plight that He said, "I hear their cries. I hear their prayers." The Lord saw every lash of the whip and how they had been taken advantage of for 400 years—and He was going to correct the injustice.

I announced, "This is how God sees the nations, including Latin countries—many of which have been through tremendous turmoil."

Then I shared with them, word for word, what I had

received at Pope John Paul II Plaza in Managua. I explained, "God told me we were to pray for one person in each family. As families are changed, the country will be changed."

I told them, "We will never reach the world by remaining within the four walls of our chapters. We must go to the people."

Then I added, "I feel impressed that we are to begin on May 4 for one week and reach out to every corner of Nicaragua." This will be the first nation.

"Nicaragua?" they questioned, with eyebrows raised. We had countries in Latin America such as Guatemala with far more chapters and stronger organizations. At the time, Nicaragua was a poor country and the Fellowship had few resources there.

Even more troubling was the fact that it was one of the most violent hot-spots in the region during those days. Nobody wanted to go there. And because of its volatile reputation, business was practically at a standstill.

Yet, this is where God told me we should go.

I'm sure some of the national presidents thought, "Whew...I'm glad God and Richard didn't pick me!"

What was the Plan?

Attending that meeting was Humberto Arguello, the national president of our Nicaraguan chapters. He is a rather reserved man who endured great persecution during the Contra wars, but none of us really knew him that well.

When I named the country, I looked over at Humberto and could almost see the heavy load that had been placed on his shoulders. Soon everyone was congratulating him, patting him on the back, saying, "We're praying for you. We will come and help you."

Later, smiling, he told me, "I feel like a bronco rider in a rodeo. Your buddies say everything will be fine, but when the chute opens and the wild bull rushes out, you are in for the ride of your life."

While we were in Miami, there were people in Nicaragua earnestly praying that God would intervene on their behalf.

I shared the objective, but I had no detailed plan of action of how we were going to reach one person in every family in Nicaragua. They returned to their home countries and began to pray for the Lord to show them how such a goal could be accomplished. They said among themselves, "Richard heard from the Lord and we are going to help him do it."

The "Fire Teams"

One by one, the men phoned me in California and committed to come to Nicaragua for a week, starting May 4, 1999. They said, "We are just business people, but there is one thing we know how to do—that is to share our personal story of how lost we were, and how through faith, our lives have been transformed."

That was the answer. In this effort there would be no big fanfare, no crusades or mass rallies, just small gatherings and one-on-one encounters. However, it would take far more than a few motivated people. There would need to be many committed Nicaraguans involved. Again, how on earth could all this come about?

Even before we were to fly in on May 4, I began hearing exciting stories of how the local chapters had developed an amazing game-plan. They formed "Fire Teams."

Those in leadership became inspired and God showed them visions of what would take place. One man reported, "I saw people at meetings in our chapters. Then the walls fell to the ground and they walked out in every direction to share their stories."

Another person was praying and saw a huge, never ending field of harvest. No matter where he looked, he could not see the end of the golden grain. The number "20" was imposed upon the field and he couldn't figure out what it meant. After more prayer, he received the answer: "This is the harvest of 20 centuries."

It was evident that this was the model Christ and the disciples used in the first century. They journeyed out from Jerusalem to city after city and saw the power of God flowing into the lives of people. Now this was being reinstated in our day.

Right on Time

When Vangie and I heard all these exciting reports, we could hardly wait to get to Nicaugra. Since May 4 was the targeted date, that's when we scheduled our plane tickets to fly from Miami to Manauga.

We had arrived in South Florida early and I said, "Why don't we catch a plane today instead of tomorrow?" I called American Airlines and was told, "Sorry, the airport in Manauga is closed. They are having a transportation strike and everything is shut down."

I learned they were burning tires in the streets and riots were springing up everywhere. This was a major concern because everything had been set for a one-week spiritual invasion starting the next day—and here we were, wondering if we could even get there at all!

I later heard that on the night before we arrived, Daniel Ortega was on national television, saying, "Only God could stop this strike." Their heels were dug in and the Sandinistas were ready to topple the government.

Early the next morning I received the news from the airlines: "The strike against the government has been called off. You can fly in today."

Vangie turned to me, "See Richard, God told you May 4, and He wouldn't let you get there one day early."

When we landed in Nicaragua, on the way to our hotel, we saw charred, burned-out buses and smoking tires smoldering all over the place. Government guards carrying loaded machine guns were positioned on every corner.

I was thankful that God had set our schedule, not man.

THE FIRE IS SPREADING

The afternoon we arrived, I was rushed off to the place

in Managua where the plans for the week were being coordinated. Boy, was I in for a shock.

Our president of Nicaragua, Humberto Arguello, showed me a computer that had the schedule for every upcoming event. Those involved were on "Fire Teams"—and hundreds of meetings had been set up in advance.

"At the end of the week we will have a record of each person we prayed with," he told me.

Humberto has an unprecedented commitment level to the Lord's work. This became obvious after the initial Fire Team outreach in Nicaragua. God knew he was the leader who would follow through—and he has never stopped. Today, he tirelessly travels the world, teaching men how to duplicate the pattern and the value of reaching every soul.

Those involved in Nicaragua were ordinary men and women representing every strata of society, and they were augmented by many who had flown in from other countries to help.

The local leaders had worked tirelessly in advance to arrange appointments and meetings in businesses, government offices, schools, universities, and a wide variety of other venues. The events were to last 30 or 40 minutes. Some were during business lunch breaks, others were at schools and universities before, after, and even during classes.

What an amazing week. The local media could hardly get enough of the story. It was front page news and during the week I was interviewed on practically every television station in the nation. Their focus was on the fact that business people were bringing a message of hope and faith.

Over 1,000 volunteers and workers were involved.

One afternoon, as I accompanied a Fire Team, we stopped at a food court for lunch. Seated at a long table, I looked down the row and saw an impressive man wearing aviator glasses. I smiled and commented, "You look like a military commander."

"I am a military commander," he quickly answered. "I am a commander in the Sandinista army."

Here was an individual who had previously burned churches, defiled villages, and had done as much hellish work as a human could possibly do. Now, because of God's grace and a total spiritual conversion, he had joined with our mission to tell others of God's love. It was another reminder that the Fellowship is not about politics or government, but something far greater.

At the end of the week, when the reports were tallied, the Fire Teams had prayed with over 97,000 men, women, and young people. But this was just the beginning.

As I write this, instead of 35 chapters in Nicaragua, there are now more than 1,100. They also have a new name: "Fishing Chapters," which have set the pattern for our worldwide success.

Today, more than 3 million of Nicaragua's 6 million citizens have been personally prayed with by Fire Team members—and the work continues. It is having a dramatic impact, and the fire is spreading!

As you will discover on these pages, the Fellowship, with over 8,000 chapters in 148 countries, has become a powerful force that is transforming nations.

Richard praying with Nicaraguan President Daniel Ortega

Personal letter from Ortega includes: "It was a great joy to know of your birthday. My sincere congratulations that Jesus keeps you in good health and energy to continue working in the noble cause of taking the message of salvation to the world...We talked with Francisco about the advances of the Fellowship in Nicaragua...I hope that we can meet soon and talk about God's message and the well-being it produces in us human beings.

Chapter 2

Escape from Kara Kala

Vangie and I were sitting at an outdoor café near Republic Square in the heart of Yerevan, the capital of Armenia. It was a picture-perfect day, framed by the gorgeous snow-capped peak of Mount Ararat in the distance—the place where Noah's Ark came to rest.

Our visit was at the invitation of the government, which is doing all it can to encourage closer business ties to the West.

We were enjoying some tea with baklava—those delicious multilayered Armenian stuffed pastries, filled with pistachio nuts and sweetened with syrup or honey. Delicious!

Suddenly, my eyes teared up. "What's wrong?" asked Vangie.

"It's okay," I answered. "I was just going back in time, remembering the incredible stories my grandfather told me about this country. I can hardly believe all that happened here—and it's bringing back a rush of memories."

THE MOLOKANS

Not too far west of Yerevan, across the Aras river in what is now Turkey, sat a small Armenian village named Kara Kala.

It was settled in the 1800s by men and women who had been exiled from central Russia and other regions because of religious persecution.

Many were Molokans—which is Russian for "milk drinkers." They earned that title in the 17th century because they refused to obey the required water-only fasting days mandated by the Russian Orthodox Church.

In Czarist Russia, these individuals who broke from the mold were viewed as heretics and soon were subject to torture, imprisonment, and eventual banishment. Thousands were sent to the Caucasus—especially Azerbaijan, Armenia, and the Ukraine.

The Tsar had another objective: he eventually offered these people free land because he wanted to establish colonies along the expanding borders of the Russian Empire. It's noteworthy that Armenia surrendered to the Russian army in 1828.

Five years later, however, something quite amazing happened. There was a spiritual revival among the Molokans, accompanied by an outpouring of the Holy Spirit as described in the Book of Acts. By the end of the 1800s their numbers had swelled to over 500,000.

The Vision

Living in a stone cottage in the small village of Kara Kala was the Klubniki family who had resettled there from Russia. One day in 1855, their 11-year-old son, Efim, suddenly had what can only be described as a supernatural vision. For seven days and nights he was under the power of God—and did not eat or sleep. He saw before him pictures, maps, charts and a written message.

Everyone in the village knew that Efim was illiterate, yet he asked for a pen and some paper and began to draw what he saw in the vision. He carefully copied the shapes of the letters and diagrams as they passed before his eyes.

When the vision was over and the manuscript was complete, the family took it to the villagers who could read. The result shocked the community. This illiterate child had written out in perfect Russian, a series of divine instructions.

He warned that at a time in the future, Kara Kala would be wiped from the face of the earth. All Armenian Christians were in extreme danger and hundreds would be brutally murdered for their faith. They must flee to a land he was being shown.

In the charts he drew a body of water. It was not the nearby Black Sea or even the Mediterranean, but the eastern edge of the United States across the far away Atlantic Ocean. The prophecy said they were not to settle there but to travel until they reached the west coast of this country. And the message concluded with this promise: "God would prosper them and make them a seed to the nations of the world."

You can imagine what a stir this caused in the village. The news spread to the entire Kars region, but many just brushed it aside as the wild ramblings of an imaginative boy and didn't pay too much attention.

Since these events were to take place "at some future time," people continued with their normal routines. Still, the family carefully preserved the unusual document.

A Son of Promise

Kara Kala eventually became home to the Shakarian family—my great-grandfather, Demos, with his wife and five daughters. This Armenian family worked a small farm and also raised cattle.

His wife, Goolisar, had become a Spirit-filled Christian and worshiped regularly with those of like faith. However, Demos was a Presbyterian, and did not fully embrace those who believed in supernatural manifestations of the Spirit of God. He would, however, visit their meetings from time to time.

If you understand the culture of this region, dating back to the times of ancient Israel, it is a stigma on a family for a mother not to produce a son. And, with five daughters, this seemed to be the lot of the Shakarians.

One day in May, 1891, Goolisar, was in the corner of

their one-room house, quietly sewing. Yet tears were streaming down her cheeks. She could no longer hold in the sadness of not being able to give birth to a son and heir to carry on the family name.

Several men had been working outside and came into the house. They saw how upset she was and Marardich Mushegan, who was a prophet, asked, "Why are you crying?"

She answered, "Because I do not have a son."

Suddenly, Maradich walked over to her and said, "Goolisar, the Lord has just spoken to me."

"Yes?" she answered.

"He has given me a message for you. One year from today you are going to be the mother of a son."

Later that afternoon, Demos came home from working in the fields and she told him the exciting news of Mushegan's announcement.

He gave her a big smile, but remained extremely skeptical of anything to do with spiritual gifts or prophecy. This did not stop him, however, from circling the date on the family calendar.

It is hard to keep good news to yourself, and soon the entire village had heard the story. Then, when Goolisar became pregnant, tongues were really wagging. Could this possibly be true?

On the exact date that was prophesied, May 25, 1892, Goolisar gave birth to a baby boy. They named him Isaac—which was appropriate, because he too was like

Abraham's son of promise.

THE SACK IN THE BARN

When my grandfather, Isaac, was about seven years old, a group of Russian Spirit-filled Christians began periodic visits to Kara Kala to enjoy fellowship with believers.

Every few months they would travel in a caravan of horse-pulled covered wagons—about 20 to a wagon.

Demos, a Presbyterian, was extremely hospitable. He could speak Russian fluently and would arrange housing for the visitors with various families.

The Russians were easy to recognize, dressed in their tunics with high collars, tied at the waist with colorful, tasseled cords. You could spot the married men—they were the ones sporting full beards.

Since Demos raised cattle, each time the visitors arrived, he would butcher a fatted steer and his family would prepare a sumptuous feast to be served. This was a huge event in Kara Kala.

"They're coming. They're coming!" announced an excited villager when he saw the caravan approaching from the distant hills.

Needing to feed at least 100 visitors, Demos picked out the finest steer he could find. This was not just for the visitors, but it was also an offering to the Lord.

This particular day he looked over the cattle and found an animal that was the fattest of the herd. There was just one problem. Due to an injury it had only one eye.

Demos was well aware that according to Scripture he was not to offer a blemished animal to the Lord but he decided that since the steer he had chosen was the largest, he could compromise just a little. He rationalized, "I'm sure God will understand."

So he went ahead and killed the animal. Then he placed the severed head in a sack which he hid beneath a large pile of hay in a corner of the barn. Next, he prepared the beef and was ready for the celebration.

How Could He Know?

When the caravan arrived there was jubilation in Kara Kala. That evening, as everyone gathered for the meal, it was time for the usual rituals. In front of long plank tables, the Shakarian family was asked to step forward and kneel to receive the blessing of one of the visiting Russian elders. Standing at the side, watching carefully, was a white-haired man, their appointed prophet.

First, the hosts were to be blessed, then the beef offering. In fact, the entire evening was one of both celebration and worship.

Appetites were heightened from the wafting aroma of the meat which was being cooked on a long spit over a huge bed of charcoal.

However, just before the prayer for the beef, the entire process came to an abrupt halt. Suddenly the prophet turned and began to walk away from the ceremony. People questioned, "What is he doing? Where is he going?"

Of course, the elder in charge didn't want to continue in the prophet's absence, so he asked those gathered to sing a hymn until he returned.

When the prophet did come back and Demos saw what was in his hand, his heart sank and he broke out in a cold sweat.

He was carrying the sack which had been hidden under the pile of threshed wheat. Then, in front of the kneeling Shakarians, the prophet opened the cloth bag and exposed the head of the steer with the blemished eye.

"Do you have anything to confess?" the old man asked.

"Yes, I do," Demos replied. "But how did you know?"

"God told me," the prophet answered."

A contrite Demos made a full confession and asked for the Lord's forgiveness. Not only did God forgive him, so did everyone present.

For the first time, he was totally convinced that the manifestations of the Holy Spirit were of God—and he personally received these spiritual gifts.

As a result of the powerful impact this made on the community, many Armenian and Russian families determined that they would never compromise with Almighty God.

Was This the Hour?

The year was 1900—the turn of a new century. It had

been 45 years since Efim, the 11-year-old received his vision from God. But since none of his writings had come true, many had decided, "He's just a false prophet."

Now 56, Efim was still living in Kara Kala when he heard a voice from heaven once more. God was telling him, "This is the time. Warn the people. What I revealed will soon come to pass."

Immediately, he rushed to every person in the village and the surrounding area, "The hour has come. Now is the time to leave the country and flee to America. It is true. Don't delay!"

He did his best to explain that unless they heeded the warning they would be faced with far more tribulation than their Russian ancestors experienced a half-century earlier. He pleaded, "Soon the door will close and leaving will be impossible."

Efim's family were among the first to flee—and they took the prophetic text with them and preserved it in a small church they established in Los Angeles.

The largest exodus, however, began after a 1904 conference of Molokan elders representing both Russian and Armenian Spirit-filled communities. The prophecy of Efim was now taken seriously and they officially supported the decision to leave.

An Uncertain Future

As each family departed, they were mocked by

unbelievers. "You are crazy, they were told. You are living a fantasy."

Why would so many Armenians ridicule them when they knew how Noah and his family were laughed at centuries earlier? All they had to do was look up at Mount Ararat and see where the ark came to rest!

Over the next few years (until 1912), hundreds of Christian families left for the west coast of America.

The Demos Shakarians made the decision in 1905, selling their possessions for whatever money they could scrape together. They made their way across the vast ocean to an uncertain future.

After arriving at New York's Ellis Island and being processed as immigrants, they found passage on a train across the continent, arriving in Southern California. What a thrill to be greeted by friends who had already made the long, tiring journey before them.

Isaac, my grandfather, was 13 years old at the time.

THE GENOCIDE

I am forever grateful that our family believed the prophecy. Those who chose to remain behind became eye witnesses and victims of one of the greatest genocides in recorded history.

In 1896, years before our family left Armenia, more than 6,000 Christians had been murdered by Muslims in Constantinople—but that city seemed so far away at the time.

The real trouble ignited in 1914 when the decision was made to totally exterminate the Christian Armenian population from the Ottoman Empire. This was carried out during World War I and involved the abduction, torture, starvation and deportation of the Armenian people. Hundreds of thousands were either slaughtered or forcibly marched to their death in the deserts of Syria.

History records the atrocities of Young Turks, including locking Christians in barns and setting them on fire. Then they would yell, "If you will accept Mohammed in place of Christ, we will open the doors."

Time after time, the committed Christians became martyrs of the faith. They chose to die, many singing hymns as the flames engulfed them.

The warning by Efim became a horrifying reality. During the genocide, every remaining inhabitant of Kara Kala was exterminated. Today, this blood-stained soil is near the site of the present Turkish village of Taslica. You can only find the original location on old Russian topographic maps of the area.

Familiar Sounds

Most of the Molokans and other Christians who escaped from the Kars region settled in what was called the "Flats," on the poor, east side of Los Angeles. The Armenians and Russians formed their own congregations, based on the villages they came from and the language they spoke. Many of the "prayer houses" were in homes.

The early Shakarians worshiped in a place that eventually became land for the I-5 Santa Ana Freeway. They named part of the new neighborhood Kara-Kala (now Boyle Heights).

Their home was at 919 Boston Street, a stucco house they shared with several Armenian families.

Times were more than tough and there was no work to be found. The family subsisted on whatever food could be spared by others in the community. The only joy was when they gathered to read Scripture, sing the praises of God, and worship in the freedom of the Spirit.

One afternoon in 1906, Demos and his brother-in-law, Marardich Muchegian (yes, the same person who had prophesied the birth of Isaac), were walking down San Pedro Street because they had heard there might be work available in a livery stable.

As they reached the corner of Azuza Street, their ears perked up as they heard familiar sounds coming from a nearby building. Following the noise, they came to a door and, in broken English, asked the man, "Can we come in?"

"Welcome, welcome," he smiled.

Inside this run-down structure were hundreds of people with their hands raised to heaven, singing, dancing, shouting, and praising God with total abandonment.

Even though they could not yet understand much of the language, they knew in their hearts this was the same Holy Spirit they had experienced back in Armenia—and how they still continued to worship in the Flats.

The Azuza Street outpouring has gone down in history as the start of the Pentecostal movement in America. It was one more manifestation of a burning fire that began in the Upper room and has never been extinguished.

Risking His Life

After being rejected for employment at every turn, Demos came home one afternoon and announced to the family, "This is a wonderful day. Thank God, I have finally found work and will be able to support you."

"Where? Where is it? What will you be doing?" his wife, daughters, and Isaac wanted to know.

After a pause, he told them that he would be joining a crew that was building a railroad line in Nevada.

"Please, no," cried Goolisar. "You will never be able to endure that heat. I hear it gets over 110 degrees there. Are you sure this is what you should do?"

Demos was far more concerned with providing for his family than any potential risk to his life. So the next day he left.

Faithfully, week after week, a money order would arrive at Boston Street—enough to feed the family and pay a little toward the rent.

Then one day the expected letter from Demos did not arrive. Sadly, the next week his body was shipped back to Los Angeles by train. He had collapsed and died while working on the rail line.

At the young age of 14, when most boys are dreaming of

their future, Isaac was now the head of the family.

Many years later, I sat down with my grandfather, Isaac, and asked, "Tell me what happened. How did you survive?"

I listened with amazement as he told me the story.

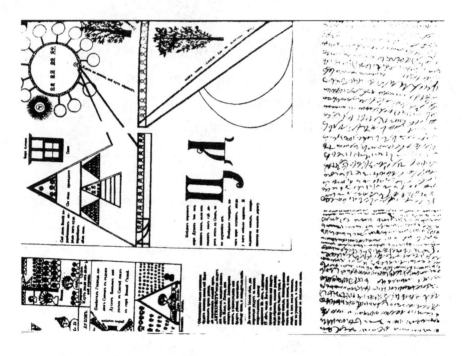

Prophecy and drawing of 11-year old Russian boy, Efim Klubniki

The original Shakarian family that came from Armenia

Chapter 3

Cows, Cows—
and More Cows!

What would become of the Shakarian family? Through a miracle of God they had escaped the genocide in Armenia, but now faced a future that was not only bleak—the situation seemed impossible.

It was hard to imagine the heartache my grandfather, Isaac, must have felt. Here he was, in a new land, with a family to take care of—and he was only fourteen years old.

"How did you survive?" I asked him. What did you do?"

I never tired of hearing his story. "I began selling newspapers on a street corner in downtown Los Angeles."

"How much did you make?" I wanted to know.

"Only about $10 a month," he answered.

I could hardly believe it. Even taking into account the fact that you could buy a loaf of bread for a nickle and a pound of sugar for four cents, the family pinched every penny and struggled to survive.

Soon Isaac spent as much time as possible at the "hiring halls" in the area, hoping and praying for anything that would pay more than selling papers. Jobs were extremely scarce and my grandfather was over the moon when he was hired by a harness factory for $15 a month.

The extra money was a godsend, yet his health soon paid the price. The fine dust he inhaled from hide-cuttings was filling his lungs and before long Isaac developed a serious cough that he couldn't shake. It racked his body night and day—and grew increasingly worse.

Isaac's cough became so serious that he was forced to see a doctor, who informed him, "Son, if you don't get out of that harness factory, you will not be alive much longer."

One evening, he returned home and was greeted by his mother with what she believed was good news. "Son, I have found a job washing and ironing for a family, so you won't have to work at the harness factory any more."

To Isaac, now 16, her words felt like a knife piercing his heart. "No," he protested, "I won't let you."

This was unthinkable. In those early days, no Armenian wife and mother worked for wages. The man of the house was the financial provider and the woman was in charge of raising the family.

This was such a grave issue that my teenage grandfather went to his room, packed his belongings in a suitcase and told his mother, "If this is your decision, I am leaving."

Goolisar sent a message to the family who had offered her work, apologizing, "I'm very sorry. I will not be able to accept the position."

THE PROMISE

One of the traditional practices of the Armenian church was for an elder or prophet to open the Bible randomly, place his finger on a Scripture verse, and read it aloud to the congregation.

On one particular Sunday, Aram Mushegan (the son of the man who had prophesied Isaac's birth back in Armenia), opened the Holy Book, pointed to a verse in the Old Testament, and read: *"Blessed shall you be in the city, and blessed shall you be in the country. Blessed shall be the fruit of your body, the produce of your ground and the increase of your herds, the increase of your cattle..."* (Deuteronomy 28:3-4).

When my grandfather heard the words "ground" and "cattle," something awakened in his spirit. "Could this possibly be the answer for me?" he wondered.

The reading continued, *"The Lord will command the blessing on you in your storehouses and in all to which you set your hand, and He will bless you in the land which the Lord your God is giving you"* (verse 8).

Isaac just knew God was speaking to him.

Even though he was practically penniless, my grandfather claimed those words for his own and walked away from his job at the harness factory.

"That had to be a brave, but scary step," I responded. "What did you do next?"

"Well, I was in a grocery store and for the first time

noticed that the vegetables and fruit looked rather stale and underdeveloped—like they had been picked before their prime. So I got the idea of going out into the farm areas and bringing fresh produce back to the city and selling door to door."

Isaac had managed to save up a few dollars for the dowery's of his sisters, so he dipped into this money to buy a used flatbed wagon and a two-year-old horse named Jack.

"Fresh-Picked Carrots!"

As the sun was rising the next morning, he headed for an area called Downey—15 miles out in the country. The trip took about three hours one way. Traveling from farm to farm, he purchased fresh produce and headed back to Los Angeles. That afternoon his voice could be heard on the streets, hollering, "Fresh-picked carrots!" "Tree-ripened oranges!" —bragging about every item in his wagon, from strawberries to spinach.

The prices were more than fair, the food was ultra fresh, and the housewives were thrilled. So much so that the next day, the women were waiting for the sight of his wagon to appear on their street.

This wasn't the only good news. Something else happened. Because of the clean, country fresh air, his lungs were being healed during those long hours on the road with Jack. Plus, during his travels, Isaac was dreaming of the day he would be able to buy a plot of land in Downey—and fulfill the Scripture he had claimed as his own. In his mind's eye he envisioned herds of cows and a thriving dairy.

At the age of 19, my grandfather had not only successfully filled the role as head of a household, he began entertaining thoughts of finding a wife and raising a family of his own.

Isaac always had a twinkle in his eye when he told me how he spotted a 15-year-old Armenian girl named Zarouhi Yessayian.

These were still the days of arranged marriages for Armenians, and since his own father had died, Isaac asked a church elder if he would be the go-between.

Of course, his future father-in-law wanted to know the goals of the man who desired his daughter's hand in marriage. "I explained how my plan was to save up enough money from my produce enterprise to buy some land and start a dairy."

He must have communicated his dreams well because the families agreed and there was a joyous celebration. God honored His promise and not long after the wedding, Isaac was able to buy ten acres of pasture land next to the San Gabriel river in Downey—and three milk cows.

Total Reliance

In 1913, while my grandparents were still building a small plankwood house on the property with their own hands, the Lord blessed them with their first child. It was a baby boy they named Demos—after Isaac's dad who had passed away working in the scorching Nevada desert. They later welcomed five daughters into their home.

Every Sunday, rain or shine, they harnessed up their buggy to Jack and clogged down the road to their Armenian church in the Flats of Los Angeles. There was much for which to praise God!

Those three cows soon became 30, then 300, and more. It was no longer a ten acre farm, but 200! The dairy was named Reliance—because they knew it was a direct result of their total reliance on the Lord.

The old frame house was replaced with an impressive two-story white stucco Spanish-style home.

Eventually, Jack was retired out to pasture—and his job was replaced by a big, black, shiny Studebaker.

Later, Isaac bought a second farm. "That gave us room for silos and automatic milking machines," my grandfather proudly told me.

During the pre-Depression years, the business expanded into hog raising, meat packing, fertilizer, and more.

Isaac never forgot the prophecy of Efim, the 11-year-old boy who decades earlier had written that God would prosper their efforts and make them a seed to the nations of the world.

As Demos grew into manhood, he worked alongside his dad. And, following in his father's footsteps, at the age of 19 his eye caught sight of a young woman in their church who captured his heart. Her name was Rose Gabrielian. Her life story paralleled that of the Shakarians, the family arriving in America with nothing and seeing her father build a prosperous garbage collection business.

Following tradition, a marriage was arranged. There were five nights of celebration, and more than 500 people attended their wedding in 1933.

The next year, I discovered America. My parents built a home next to Isaac's on the farm, and this is where I was raised, along with my brother, Stephen, and sister Geraldine.

BLESSED IN A TIME OF FAMINE

The Great Depression had a devastating impact on the nation, yet during those difficult days, the Shakarian empire continued to grow. There were now three dairy farms and over 3,000 cows.

In addition, Isaac helped several of his brother-in-laws start businesses—including the Great Western Milk Transport Company, which featured 500 milk tankers used to help transport our dairy products throughout the state. Also, the Great Western Packing Company, which slaughtered 700-800 cattle daily. It was run by Tom Kardashian (who married Isaac's youngest sister, Hamas).

He is the grandfather of the well-known attorney, Robert Kardashian.

Reliance Dairy Farms eventually became the largest independently owned dairy in the world.

What was written long ago about the son of Abraham had come true for a Californian named Isaac. He too was blessed in a time of famine (Genesis 26).

Valuable Training

Our family definitely displayed the gift of hospitality, and even though I was very young during the Great Depression, I can still remember how my mom and grandmother lovingly took care of the hungry transients who showed up at our door. They were great cooks and always shared Armenian food with those in need.

What a wonderful childhood I enjoyed. I loved growing up on a farm—riding real horses as I played cowboys and Indians with my friends. We hid behind haystacks pretending to shoot each other. Later, I learned to drive by bumping an old pickup truck into those haystacks.

From as early as I can remember, faith was central to our lives. It involved far more than attending the Armenian church on Sunday, the things of God were talked about daily in our home—and in our business.

Because of building such a successful enterprise, my grandfather became an important sought-after voice in the high circles of the day. People came from miles away to seek his counsel and ask his favor—including government officials, owners of corporations, and wealthy investors.

I can clearly recall the gatherings in his home. After a sumptuous spread of food, the men would gather in the front room, with my grandfather sitting in a big chair by the fireplace.

I was just seven years of age, but he would say, "Richard, come here and stand by me. Tell these men about Jesus."

It was his way of sharing the Gospel—and I didn't hesitate to present a short, simple message of faith. Then he would add, "You know, Richard is going to be used to bring the Gospel to many people."

Although I was unaware of the fact, I was receiving valuable early training, equipping me with the ability to communicate with leaders.

My father and grandfather were not typical farmers or dairymen; I never saw either one of them in coveralls. At work they always dressed in business suits and presented themselves as professionals.

The small office in which they worked was able to house two desks face to face, one for my dad and one for my grandfather, Isaac. They both felt they could make better decisions working together.

Anti-Aircraft Guns

The eventful day of December 7, 1941, changed everything. President Roosevelt announced on the radio that Pearl Harbor had been attacked and we were at war with Japan.

Not many days later, a convoy of U.S. Army vehicles drove onto our property. Curious, I followed them as they went to the back of our dairy and set up anti-aircraft guns.

Wow! For a seven-year-old this was exciting. I knew we had special cows, but didn't think they were *that* valuable!

It turned out that they were there to protect the North American Aviation plant situated about a mile and a half away. They had a contract with the government to produce combat planes during World War II.

We knew things were serious when our grammar school built a bomb shelter and covered it with grass. It had two long rows of benches, enough for all the students in case of an attack. Those drills made me nervous.

As a youngster, and into middle school, I always loved to read my Bible and spent far more time praying than did others my age. I never felt I would become a minister, but the Lord was very real to my life and I just wanted to be as close to Him as possible.

I could not explain the feeling, but in my heart was a passion to share the love of God with everyone I met.

Earthquake in the Haystack

Late one afternoon, my mother was calling me in for dinner, but I didn't answer. When dad arrived home she asked, "Honey, will you go out and find Richard. I have no idea where he is."

He finally spotted me, perched on top of an 8-foot-tall haystack, talking with our gardener Zarope, who spoke fluent Armenian—as did I.

To me, Zarope was a notorious sinner who really needed to know the Lord, but wasn't quite ready. So in my youthful exuberance I was going to put a little pressure on him.

As the California sun was setting, I said, "Zarope, it's going to be a night like this when the angel of the Lord is going to come down from the sky and put one foot on the sea, one foot on the land, and blow the trumpet. There will be a mighty earthquake and Jesus is going to return."

By this time, my father had quietly sneaked up and was hiding behind the haystack, listening to every word. The minute I uttered the word "earthquake," he grabbed those bales of hay with both hands and began shaking them violently.

Zarope literally jumped into the air, almost out of his skin, exclaiming, "My God, it's the end of the world. Jesus help me!"

We made a believer out of him in a hurry!

From My Head to My Heart

It was a real turning point when, as a 12-year-old, I was invited to attend a Christian youth camp in the San Bernardino mountains.

Late one evening, when the other kids were either in the recreation hall or already in bed, I felt an overwhelming urge to receive everything the Lord had for me. So I went to the chapel and began praying—alone.

It was there, around midnight, I had what I can only describe as a vision of Jesus. At first I saw just His feet, but I soon realized He was standing before me. He placed His hand on my head and something amazing happened.

As a youngster, because of the massacres that occurred in Armenia, our love for Christ was measured by the decision we would make if someone was about to kill us for our faith. The choice was based on our mindset.

But this night all of that changed. My love for the Lord fell out of my head and dropped into my heart. The only way I can describe what took place is that Jesus touched me and now I was truly in love with Him.

I knew nothing of theology, I just cared about Jesus, and He filled me with His Holy Spirit.

When I walked out of the chapel, my whole world had changed. The sky was painted with stars, and the distant lights of Southern California seemed to be twinkling His love.

My heart was overflowing with His presence and I couldn't wait to get back to Downey.

For years, I had been bold about sharing my faith, but now I was bubbling over.

A Message for Mr. Sachs

When my dad walked into the Bank of America where he did business, his banker told him, "Demos, do you know that your son came in here recently and prayed with me?"

Dad wasn't surprised.

Every day, as I walked home from school I passed the Sachs Ford-Lincoln-Mercury dealership and developed a deep desire to pray for the owner.

Apprehensively, I walked in, spoke with the secretary and said, "I would like an appointment with Mr. Sachs."

She knew our family and asked, "When?"

"How about tomorrow afternoon?" I answered.

The next day I was ushered into Mr. Sachs' office and he was very gracious. "What do you want to see me about?" he asked.

I glanced around his office and on the walls were displayed the stuffed heads of several animals he had shot—so I was determined not to make a mistake in my presentation!

I hadn't prepared a speech, but after stammering around for a few seconds, I blurted out, "Mr. Sachs, every time I pray your face comes to my mind. I just came here to say that Jesus really loves you and to pray for you"—which I did.

Then I left and walked home.

Several weeks later, I passed his house, which wasn't too far from ours. He was out in the garden taking care of some flowers. Even though I didn't stop to chat, I thought, "This is really odd, a businessman at home, gardening in the middle of a workday."

Not long after, I learned that Mr. Sachs had died of cancer. I'm so grateful that in God's perfect timing He allowed me to pray with this gentleman.

"Don't Just Sit There!"

Sharing my faith eventually led to starting a Bible Club. My initial reason being that three of my buddies didn't know the Lord and I wanted them to have a relationship with God.

My plan worked. And now I had a team.

During those days, a man named Fred Jordan was having a strong impact on the region through his Soul Clinic ministry. This was a program to teach people how to reach others with their faith—something I was already doing, but I longed to learn more.

My dad informed me, "Richard, they don't accept young people." Not easily discouraged, I replied, "Well, since you are donating free milk to his mission program, please take me there and let me ask Mr. Jordan personally. If he turns me down, that's okay, but at least let me try."

Mr. Jordan not only let me be part of the training, he also welcomed three other high school students. I was the youngest in attendance.

At one point the four of us were in the chapel when Fred Jordan opened the door. We were seated in the front row and he asked, "What are you talking about today?"

I told him, "School is about to start and we are trying to figure out how to reach more kids."

He smiled and said, "You're in the wrong position."

"What do you mean?" I asked, a little confused.

"Don't just comfortably sit there, get down on your knees and pray."

We quickly did as he suggested and God inspired us with a plan for starting more Bible Clubs. In addition to our weekly meeting, we called Saturdays "Field Day." This is when we would work with young people from various churches to witness in Los Angeles. We would climb on the streetcars and share Christ with the passengers on board, and meet shoppers on street corners. This was meeting a real need. Young people loved what we were doing and the Bible Clubs began to multiply.

Friday Night Live!

When I was 13 Fred Jordan telephoned me with a request, "You guys are doing such a phenomenal job, why don't you take our 15 minute Friday night radio program on KGER and report to our audience what is happening. This was all before Christian television hit Southern California.

The four of us, who were leading the Bible Clubs, made a pact with each other. No one could be on the program unless they had personally led an individual to the Lord that week—or unless a guest was a new convert that week. We wanted only current testimonies.

Fred Jordan allowed us to have this time slot for three years and I never missed being on the program which became extremely popular.

The results were amazing. Over 300 Bible Clubs were launched—not just in California, but all over the country and as far away as Australia.

Because of this, I was invited to fly to Washington, D.C. to speak to the Congressional Prayer Group. These elected officials wholeheartedly supported what we were doing to positively change and influence the lives of young people.

Where would all this lead? At the time, my father was deeply involved in the family dairy business, but his future was about to dramatically change.

Rose, Demos, and baby Richard

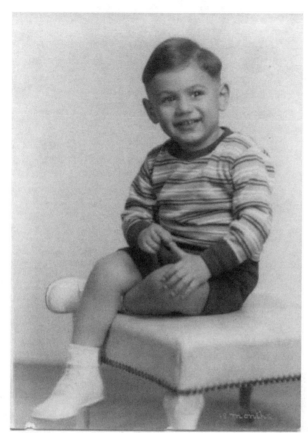

Little Richard

Reliance Dairy, Downey, California

Chapter 4

Much More than Business

Reliance Dairy was booming and business absorbed more and more of my father's time, yet his heart was troubled.

One night in prayer, he confessed to God that he had been drifting away from what truly mattered. Under deep conviction, he totally rededicated his life—and his future—to the Lord.

While the expansion of the dairy would continue, he made a commitment to spend every spare moment possible sharing his faith.

What role could he play? What could he do? After all, my dad didn't consider himself to be a public speaker, he was simply a businessman with a burden.

Starting the following year, dad began sponsoring a number of evangelists who held tent crusades in Southern California.

Uncle Gabriel's

Around this time, my father struck up a warm, personal friendship with Dr. Charles S. Price—a former Congregational minister who had a huge following because he truly believed in the "full gospel"—that miracles, signs, and wonders, were not limited to the New Testament church, but were for believers today.

Price, who lived in Pasadena, California, often drove to Downey to have lunch with my dad at Uncle Gabriel's Log Cabin Restaurant. He loved the place—with its rustic wooden tables and sawdust floors. They would even let you pick fresh oranges and peaches from the trees on their property!

I was allowed to tag along and would sit there absorbing the wisdom of this great man of God.

Every few months our family drove to the home of Dr. Price, a trip I really looked forward to. An added attraction being that in his house was a large cage which housed a couple of monkeys.

I can still remember the morning he told my parents, "I believe God is going to use your son, Richard, in a special way." This was before I began my youth outreach described in the previous chapter.

One summer night, my dad took Dr. Price to hear a noted evangelist holding meetings in Los Angeles. The man preached hell, fire, and brimstone until sinners almost felt the flames and came rushing to the altar for salvation.

Driving back to Pasadena, my dad was gushing with

excitement, "That sermon was really powerful," he said.

Dr. Price was quiet for a moment, then commented, "Demos, that is not the message of the future. The world is longing to hear about God's love, His compassion, and the gifts of the Spirit—a truth that will be accompanied by great waves of healing and salvation."

He prophesied that a revival would sweep America—not sparked by denominations or well-known preachers—but springing from ordinary men and women who would come from nowhere and accomplish amazing exploits for God.

His words became true. In the mid-to-late 1940s, huge crusades were in the headlines across America, and countless thousands were finding Christ.

A $3,000 Budget?

In 1948, when I was 14 and having such a remarkable response with our Bible Clubs and radio broadcast, a group of pastors felt it was high time to hold a giant youth rally in Los Angeles. So they decided to book the Shrine Auditorium—which, at the time, rented for just a few hundred dollars. Since they didn't have the money, someone suggested they contact Demos Shakarian to help raise the funds.

My dad was always thinking in big terms, and suggested they increase their budget to $3,000 so they could really promote the event with radio and newspaper ads.

My father decided to invite 100 businessmen for a free dinner at Knott's Berry Farm in Buena Park—with the understanding that an offering would be taken to sponsor the area-wide youth rally.

I'll never forget that night. On the spur of the moment, my father thought it might be a good idea if a few of the men would come to the microphone and share their turning point of how Christ had helped them. One after another —for the next hour and a half—we listened to stories of restored marriages, deliverance from alcoholism, addictions, and much more. Emotions ran high and there was hardly a dry eye in the place.

My dad finally told those in attendance, "Friends, we've just heard the full gospel...from businessmen." Those words were to have a special meaning for him in the days ahead.

When the offering was received, the cash and checks totaled an amazing $6,200. Far more than expected!

The rally packed the Shrine Auditorium, with hundreds outside who couldn't get in. When it was over, along with the offering taken that night, there was a fund established that now exceeded $5,000.

Thrilled and encouraged, my dad decided to take it one step further and the leaders booked the 20,000-seat Hollywood Bowl for a Monday night youth rally. It was jammed to capacity, with another 2,500 standing around the edges of the amphitheater.

It was just one year later that Billy Graham held his historic tent meeting in Los Angeles and our family did everything possible to promote the event. As a fifteen-year-old, I was amazed to see so many people giving their lives to Christ.

Reliance Dairy was expanding on all fronts, but our family remained committed to sponsoring major evangelistic events.

Mustard Seed Faith

In late September, 1951, dad arranged for Oral Roberts to erect his giant tent in Los Angeles. Over 200,000 attended during the 16 nights.

Just to be a helper in God's work made my father feel like he was one of the happiest people on earth!

One of my perks was to drive Oral from his hotel to the meetings each night. This was heady stuff for a young man—and I had no idea how Roberts would play a key role in my future.

Late one evening, my dad was having a cup of coffee and a piece of pie with the evangelist at a local diner. "Oral," he began, "I'd like to share something that's been burning on my heart."

Roberts listened as my dad talked about starting an organization where ordinary businessmen would gather together and tell personal stories of God's work in their lives. He had not seen many men active in the Lord's work.

"How would it grow?" Roberts wanted to know.

"Well, one man would tell others and invite them to the meetings," explained my father.

"What are you going to call the organization?" asked Oral.

My dad was way ahead of him on this point and had it all

figured out. Recalling what happened at Knott's Berry Farm—and adding more to it—he said, "It's going to be named the Full Gospel Business Men's Fellowship International."

Since it hadn't even begun, the word *International* seemed a little presumptuous, but dad was convinced this was the right name.

Oral became excited about the idea and climbed on board, asking, "How can I help?"

Since the big tent meeting was drawing to a close, dad thought the idea would really take off if Oral could be the featured speaker at the first gathering. So he quickly contacted Clifton's Cafeteria, a popular spot on the corner of Broadway and Seventh in downtown Los Angeles. They had a second floor dining room that was available on Saturday mornings.

Things were falling neatly into place. This was going to be huge! My father phoned every businessman he knew and gave them a personal invitation. "Bring a few friends with you, he encouraged. It's going to be wonderful."

Dad was filled with anticipation when he drove to the venue with my mom and Oral that second Saturday of October, 1951. They were running a little late and my father wondered, "How many will show up? Two hundred? Three hundred? Perhaps even more?"

When they reached the top of the stairs and looked around they questioned if they had the right room. After they counted heads, only 18 men were present. What a major disappointment!

Trying to make the best of a bad situation, dad tried to convey the idea for the organization—"Just one man telling another about the Lord."

He turned the meeting over to Oral, who talked for 20 minutes on the topic of mustard seed faith—how great things start from small beginnings. He concluded with these words, "Lord, Jesus, let this Fellowship grow in Your strength alone. Send it marching in Your power across the nation and around the world. Lord, we see a little group of people in a cafeteria, but You see a thousand chapters."

Was This the End?

My mom and dad left, still excited, but their enthusiasm was surely tested. I began helping them with the Saturday morning meetings—mainly so there would be as many warm bodies present as possible. I was in charge of setting up the microphones and tape recording equipment.

But the crowds remained small. Some days 15 would show up, and on a good morning, there might be 40.

Dad even broadcast the meetings live on KGER radio and on a Mexican station that blasted its signal to half the United States. Nothing seemed to light the needed fuse of fire.

That summer, because of leading youth activities in Southern California, I was invited to speak in Cuba. At the time, Fidel Castro was threatening a military coup and the atmosphere was highly controlled. Machine guns were visible everywhere, but wherever I spoke, the people were extremely receptive. It was my first trip to a foreign nation and it gave me a hunger to reach more of the world for Christ.

On my return, dad invited me to tell my experiences at one of his Clifton Cafeteria chapter meetings.

It would be wonderful to report that the organization dad began was now firmly on its feet and flourishing, but that was not the case. The Saturday before Christmas, 1952, there were fewer people attending than when it began, 14 months earlier.

That morning, a few of dad's most loyal friends and supporters kindly suggested, "Demos, I think it might be time to give up on this idea. I don't believe it's going anywhere."

This was perhaps the saddest Christmas my dad ever experienced. It was now Friday night, and the next morning he would be announcing to the small gathering that this was the final meeting of the Fellowship.

It was more than his heart could bear. So he slipped away from the dinner table and found a place to get alone with God. There, even though he was on bended knees, on his Persian carpet in the living room, he suddenly felt his spirit rising. It was as if he was being lifted above the house—and could see over the rooftops of Downey. Soon, in this vision from heaven, he was raised high enough to view the mountains, the sea, and finally the whole earth.

In his own words, "I could see people around the world—their race, and color of their skin. And like a zoom camera can show minute details from a distance, I could see people close together. Every face was rigid, wretched, locked in his own private death."

My dad was frightened at the implication—billions of

lost souls. He cried out, "Lord, please save them!"

In a flash, God showed him these same people with faces glowing, raising their hands toward heaven. And he heard the Lord tell him, "My son, the very thing you see before you will soon come to pass."

My dad rose to his feet totally recharged—a new man. This vision was what he would now share with the men the next morning.

When he walked in the room, an officer of the organization, Miner Arganbright, handed him an envelope. It was obviously going to be a letter of resignation. Instead, to my father's surprise, it contained a check for $1,000. The gentleman explained, "God woke me up last night and said this work must continue."

Another person present, Thomas Nickel, hailed from San Francisco. He had only been to one previous meeting, but God impressed upon him to get in his car, drive all night to Los Angeles and offer his printing presses to start a national magazine for the Fellowship.

This was not the death, but an amazing resurrection of the organization. Soon, hundreds were attending. New chapters were popping up across the country and the first national convention was in the planning process.

The words of Dr. Price and Oral Roberts were coming true!

I Was Smitten!

Earlier that fall, I enrolled as a freshman at a small Christian college in Costa Mesa that is now Vanguard

University. I tried living in the dorms for the first semester, but this was difficult since I had been given more and more responsibilities at the dairy. I was named head of the sales department, a big step up from my earlier days running the bottle washer and other messy jobs.

With my new assignment, I decided it would be easier to live at home and commute the 28 miles each way.

As a young, single guy, I admit I had a weakness for fancy cars, and was proud to drive my new Corvette to campus. It didn't last long. One evening, horsing around with some buddies, we were street racing and I totaled the vehicle in an accident. Fortunately, I lived to tell about it—and to buy another car.

This time it was a new Buick Century convertible. Red, with white trim, plenty of shiny chrome, red leather seats, and Italian spoke wheels.

This is what I was driving when I pulled onto campus to register for classes the second semester of my junior year—January, 1955. Across the room I couldn't help but notice a tall, stunning girl, accompanied by her father. Obviously, she was new, or I would have surely seen her before!

I didn't know it at the time, but as she was leaving with her dad, she spotted my car and was curious who was getting into it.

In the dorms, evidently my name came up and some of the girls told this new coed that I worked at a family business in Downey—"We'll introduce you if you'd like to meet him."

In between classes one morning, I met this tall, Scandinavian girl named Vangie Klingsheim.

In ten seconds flat, I was totally smitten!

On a Minnesota Farm

I learned Vangie was full-blooded Norwegian. Her mother, a woman named Elizabeth Haukland, was born and raised in the picturesque village of Moi, Norway, not far from the city of Stavanger. While still a teenager, Elizabeth began attending a Bible study and felt a call to go to China as a missionary. So, in her early 20s, she and a girlfriend waved goodbye to their families and followed their hearts.

On the long trip, they traveled to America and stopped in a small community in southern Minnesota near Spring Valley. The family had contact with several Norwegians who had previously moved there. After a Sunday morning church service the girls were invited to dinner at the farm of Olav Klingsheim and his wife, who were the parents of seven boys and a daughter.

One of the sons, Oscar, also had a call to ministry, so he and Elizabeth found plenty to talk about.

The young women continued on their journey to China, and for the next four years, Elizabeth and Oscar wrote each other constantly. You can probably guess the outcome. When she returned, they were married—and planned to go back to the Orient as missionaries. However, the political situation in China had escalated from bad to worse, and Oscar began pioneering churches in Minnesota, later becoming a pastor in Washington, Oregon, and Montana.

Along the way, they raised a family—a daughter Naomi, a son Phil, and a daughter named Evangeline, whom everyone called Vangie.

"Why can't I graduate from high school early and start college in January?" the high school senior asked her principal in Kalispell, Montana. "After all, I have all the credits needed."

Vangie's request was not only granted, but she would be able to return the next spring to graduate with her class.

She chose the college in Costa Mesa because it was close to her married sister and brother who had moved to California.

Prime Rib in Beverly Hills

It was a Friday night. After working in the sales lane of one of our drive-in dairy stores, I was feeling rather sorry for myself. I wanted to be with Vangie.

Walking behind the creamery into the barn where the milking was being done, I stared into the big brown eyes of one of the cows and thought, "Richard, you are a fool. You should be looking into the beautiful green eyes of Vangie!"

My parents were out of town, so the next morning I walked through the rose arbor that connected our house with grandfather Isaac's and started talking with my aunt Florence, who was there having breakfast. I told her, "There's a girl I want to take out, but I don't know how to go about it, or where to go."

"That shouldn't be a problem" she smiled. "Let me help you."

Good to her word, she scoured through the newspaper and found a concert we both might like—and arranged for the tickets. I quickly phoned Vangie and she accepted my invitation.

Following the concert I took Vangie to the world-famous Lawry's Restaurant in Beverly Hills. It's a hangout for film stars where the waiters carve prime rib at your table. My date was really impressed.

My Heart was Beating Fast

When I saw how the guys on campus were looking at my girl, I decided I had better act quickly. So in March, just two months after we met, I took Vangie to dinner in Laguna Beach. Then, I drove up to a high hill overlooking the Pacific Ocean and parked the car. With my heart barely able to contain the love and happiness I was feeling, I plucked up enough courage to pop the question: "Will you marry me?"

Vangie was in shock. At 18, and a freshman in college, she certainly wasn't thinking marriage. "I'll have to ask my parents first," she told me.

Our family had one mutual friend of the Klingsheims, an evangelist named Velmer Gardner. So late one evening my dad picked up the phone and called him—not realizing he was in the east and it was the middle of the night. Getting right to the point, he asked, "Velmer, what do you think about Richard marrying Vangie Klingsheim?"

Half awake, he mumbled, "Sounds good to me! Great family," and that was it. I'm sure he just wanted to get off the phone and back to his pillow.

Before Vangie's parents came down to Southern California in May, her sister, Naomi, warned her Norwegian mother, "You need to know that Richard is Armenian and rather dark complected." On hearing this news, they didn't know what to expect!

After what seemed like an eternity, the day came for me to officially ask Vangie's father for her hand in marriage. A caravan of cars with my parents and grandparents headed to Culver City, at the home of Vangie's sister where her family was staying. I will never forget the scene. The men congregated in one room, the women in another, and Reverend Klingsheim was giving me a hard time over what was about to happen—all in good fun, of course.

I finally got around to asking his permission and breathed a sigh of relief when he said, "Yes." Vangie and I were beyond happy.

As was our family tradition, it was time for another celebration. Immediately, my parents threw an engagement party on the grounds of our estate—huge charcoal pits with shish-kabobs, rice pilaf, and tasty Armenian side dishes. A special guest was Lillian Thrasher—a renowned missionary to Egypt, known as "The Mother of the Nile" for her selfless work with orphans.

When Vangie looked out the window and caught sight of 300 guests seated around a giant elm tree, she felt intimidated—especially since she hardly knew any of our extended family and friends. She need not have worried. When she appeared, wearing a gorgeous dress, she was the star of the show and the light of my life.

What Would the Elders Think?

The next Sunday I proudly took Vangie to our Armenian church for the first time. She had never seen women sitting on one side of the congregation and men on the other. The benches had no backs. The elders—some with long beards—sat in the front corner, and before them was a table covered with a white cloth and an oversized Bible. The head elder in those days was my grandfather, Isaac.

At that time, most of the church members had not married outside the culture, so heads really turned when my fair-skinned Norwegian wife-to-be walked into the small sanctuary.

Vangie had never heard Scriptures sung in a minor key in Armenian; this was all brand new to her. After the service, I was thrilled that the people I had grown up with embraced and welcomed her with open arms.

Back to Kalispell

There was another matter on the checklist. Vangie was determined to graduate with her high school class in Kalispell, so she and her family returned to Montana. I was sure glad there was an engagement ring on her finger —letting everyone know this girl was spoken for.

A few days later, I drove my convertible to Kalispell and

we headed for Denver, Colorado, where my parents were leading the third international convention of the Fellowship. The organization was growing—and so was our family.

THE GETAWAY!

The wedding date was set for August 6, 1955. To accommodate the several hundred guests, it was held at the stately First Presbyterian Church in Downey. Vangie's father, reverend Klingsheim, and Fred Jordan officiated—but when I saw Vangie walking down the aisle, she took my breath away. I can't remember another word spoken from that moment on.

The reception was at the Rio Hondo Country Club, and I heard that some of the Armenian guys planned to kidnap my bride—probably to get even for the many pranks we had played on them over the years.

The clubhouse was set back from the road about 300 yards and there was a single lane in and out. So thinking ahead, my friend Ralph and I devised an escape plan. Across the golf course was a concrete riverbed which was dry in the summer.

A reflective tape called Scotchgard had just come on the market, and we carefully marked several trees leading to the river. Then we cut the wire fence at the edge of the property, ready for our get-away in Ralph's car. We even did a test run in the river bed to see how fast we could drive and where there was an up-ramp that would get us to the Santa Ana Freeway.

I had already booked the honeymoon suite at the Hilton

in downtown Los Angeles. So the morning of the wedding, I put our suitcases in the trunk of my convertible, drove it to the Pershing Square car garage near the hotel, hid the ticket in my shoe, and Ralph drove me back to Downey.

To further disguise our plan, Ralph borrowed a car from the local Buick agency, carefully parked it at the back door of the club house, and blocked off the service roads on each side.

Despite our best efforts, the plan failed. Since this was the only vehicle back there, the pranksters knew which car to target. So while the toasts and speeches were going on inside, Ralph whispered in my ear, "They've opened the hood and pulled out all the ignition wires!"

"No problem," I responded. "Look at your watch. Pull your car back there in exactly 30 minutes and we'll make our getaway." Meanwhile the Armenian pranksters were out front, revving up their engines—waiting for some real action.

"It's time," I finally told Vangie. "Let's go!"

Ralph and his girlfriend, Shirley, had pulled their vehicle around to the rear and we literally dove into the back seat.

However, one fast-acting fellow reached in and grabbed the keys and we were soon surrounded by their cars. After a couple of minutes of this standoff, I said, "Tell you what. We can have a lot more fun if you give Ralph those keys, and then you can chase us."

They believed me, hurried to the front, and waited to give chase.

"Step on it!" I told Ralph. Across the golf course we

sped, following the glow-marked trees. With the girls screaming, we drove through the clipped wire fence, down into the riverbed, and up onto the I-5 freeway to our honeymoon getaway.

Those confused guys spent the next hour rushing around Downey in circles—scratching their heads in disbelief at our disappearing act.

Thousands of Customers

Before our marriage, Reliance had created an entirely new retail marketing concept, the drive-thru dairy store —and it became my responsibility to make it succeed.

It was "fast food" before its time. People would pull up to a window, place there order for milk, ice cream, bread, bacon, or a dozen other products, and in less than a minute we would hand them their order.

The stores grew from one, to ten, to nearly 30 in Southern California—and I was responsible for over 400 employees.

Because our prices were cheaper, we were nearly wiping out the old-fashioned home milk delivery routes and attracting thousands of customers daily.

Our promotions became legendary. I purchased plastic buckets, filled them with a variety of products and sold them for $.99 or $1.99—and the bucket was free!

We also began offering free pony rides to the kids of our customers, and had a stable of 30 ponies in the process.

I even got the idea to print a black and red mailer with

four discount coupons—items people needed such as eggs, ice cream, or cottage cheese. These were distributed to homes within a one mile radius of each store. When we tabulated the results, there was one coupon redeemed for every mailer we sent. An unbelievable response!

We decided to run special midnight sales, with greatly slashed prices on certain items from 8:00 P.M. until the clock struck 12.

Vangie and I drove to one of our stores to check on the sales. Cars were lined up for a quarter-mile before they even reached the property. I phoned our other locations and it was gang-buster traffic everywhere. The highway patrol was soon complaining that we were blocking the exit ramp off a major freeway!

One year, just before a Christmas when the economy was in a severe recession, I decided to help needy families in our community. So I printed 1,000 gift food coupons—each good for three oversized shopping bags stuffed full of basic food supplies, plus a turkey.

I phoned several of our suppliers and told them what we were doing. "We really need your help. What can you donate for this outreach?" I had the promise of 1,000 packs of hot dogs, 1,000 loaves of bread, and much more.

Here's the problem I faced. How would these be fairly distributed?

The answer was to invite 50 people who worked with community non-profit organizations that dealt with underprivileged families. During a free lunch at a hotel, I told them of the plan. After showing a sample of the food bags, I said, "It will be your decision who receives them. There is a form for your name, your organization, and the name of the person you are giving it to. Our clerks will take the form, and present the food."

Then I added, "Before you leave, I want to introduce you to a friend of mine. My guest was Nicky Cruz—a former gang member in New York whose story was the theme of the movie, "Cross and the Switchblade," starring Pat Boone.

Cruz told how the love of God did for him what judges, prison, and psychologists couldn't do. His was a powerful message that set the perfect tone for reaching out to those who were hurting not only materially, but spiritually.

Time to Get Our Passports

Since Reliance Dairy Farms stores were never open on Sunday, Vangie and I were constantly speaking at special events—with an emphasis on youth.

Plus, we were blessed to be starting a family of our own with the birth of two daughters, Denice and Cynthia.

"Lord, what are you trying to tell me?" I asked as I was praying in 1959. I began getting out of bed and praying in the night, feeling God was going to send us somewhere overseas.

I confided to my father that we would be traveling to different nations. "I don't know just where," I told him.

Just in case, we applied for and received our passports.

I had no idea what was about to happen next.

Richard, age 18, speaking at Clifton's Cafeteria, the original FGBMFI chapter

Richard's first car, given to him by his grandfather

Richard and Vangie's engagement day at grandpa Isaac's home

Little Vangie

Vangie's mother, Elizabeth, in China.
Right, with Chinese orphan, 1924

China dress worn by
Vangie's mother

Vangie's parents, Rev. and
Mrs. Oscar Klingsheim

CHAPTER 5

EIGHTY AMAZING DAYS

It was my dad on the phone. "Richard, what are you and Vangie doing tomorrow night?"

"Why?" I answered. "What's up?"

"Well, Oral Roberts is flying in from Tulsa and he's joining us for dinner at the house. I was wondering if you could come over?" Of course we would! It was the early spring of 1960.

We were sitting in the living room after the meal, when Oral looked at me and said, "Richard, our evangelistic association is making plans to send a youth team around the world to reach a new generation with the Gospel. You and Vangie are under consideration to be included." Then he added, "Please, understand that nothing has been decided, but if you are chosen, you'll have to get your passports."

He was totally surprised when I responded, "We already have our passports,"—as if someone had already tipped us off to his plans.

Then I explained, "Oral, I have no idea what you've been

working on, but for several months, the Lord has been waking me up in the middle of the night, telling me that we would be making a major trip overseas. In fact, I've been so convinced of this that we have even made arrangements for someone else to take my place managing the drive-in dairy stores. Plus, Vangie's parents have agreed to take care of our girls."

At the time, Denice was three-and-a-half, and Cynthia was 18 months old.

I didn't hesitate to let him know, "I'm not sure if the trip you are referring to is what God has been speaking to me about. If it is, so be it, but if not, I know the Lord has something else in store."

A Whirlwind Summer

A few days later, we were excited to receive the official invitation and I was slated to be the speaker at all the events.

This was the first "Abundant Life Youth Team" scheduled to conduct over 200 meetings in 27 countries during the coming summer. The theme was "Around the World in 80 Days"—chosen because of the popular movie of the same name starring Noel Coward and David Niven.

It was a four-month commitment that included four weeks of preparation in Tulsa during the month of May before the actual journey began. In addition to Vangie and me, members of the team included Neil Eskelin, his sister

LuWayne, and Mary Hazelton. There would be dramatic presentations and music geared to break language barriers and appeal to children and youth.

It was heart-wrenching to say goodbye to our daughters as we boarded the plane for the first leg of our global adventure, but we knew they were in safe and loving hands.

Vangie had never been out of the country before and wasn't quite sure what to pack. For example, after our first meetings in Puerto Rico, we were preparing to check out of the hotel to catch a flight to South America. Vangie was running late, and the man who traveled with the team and made all the arrangements, grabbed her travel bag. In the rush, it flew open and all the contents tumbled to the floor— including 10 large tubes of toothpaste.

"What's all this for?" he asked in disbelief.

Vangie innocently answered, "Oh, I just wanted to be prepared."

He smiled, "I'll let you in on a secret. They sell toothpaste in every city of the world." We all laughed!

BEDBUGS!

Our second destination was Barrancabermeja, Columbia —in the north-central part of that country, where we were to conduct several giant youth rallies.

We had seen a picture of the hotel where we were booked to stay, but when we arrived, it certainly didn't live up to its promotion and was sadly lacking by U.S.

standards. The swimming pool was pitch black in color—it looked like greasy oil. You wouldn't want to stick your toe in there, let alone your body!

When we were shown to our room, the small twin beds were literally crawling with tiny dark bugs. "I'm not laying down there," Vangie protested. "I'll just sleep standing up."

That night, exhausted after our travels, she finally gave in and bravely brushed every bug off one of the little beds and prayed over it, "Lord, protect us!"

Vangie told me, "You and I are going to sleep on this one together." I guess she only had faith for one bed!

When the sun arose, our bed was bug-free, while the other was still swarming with creepy-crawlies!

East and West

"Around the World in 80 Days" was a hectic, but spiritually rewarding experience.

Our fifth wedding anniversary was celebrated in Berlin, Germany, where the youth meetings were scheduled for three nights in a giant tent, not far from the dividing line between the East and West. Some people in attendance were from communist East Berlin (the heavily guarded Berlin Wall was constructed one year later).

During that visit we were invited to meet with the mayor of Berlin. Even though he held a secular position, we spoke to him openly concerning spiritual matters. We had no idea that this gentleman would eventually become the Chancellor of West Germany and Nobel Peace Prize winner—Willy Brandt.

It's the Police!

In India, the crowds attending our youth rallies were large and very receptive. They were held in soccer fields and other open air venues in Trivandrum, Tirunelveli, Nagercoil, Madras (now renamed Chennai).

In one village we were staying in a travelers' bungalow. The accommodations were rugged, to say the least—with an open hole in the floor for the toilet.

Before we could settle down, the manager came to our room and said, "The police are here and they want to talk with you."

"No problem," I told him.

I invited the two men in and offered them a soft drink. "How can I be of help?" I wanted to know.

Immediately, one gentleman began questioning me about specific places and the exact times where we had been during the previous few days. It was obvious our whereabouts were being logged and we were being followed. These men were working for India's internal security, the equivalent of the FBI.

They let me know that it was against the law to preach (or proselytize) in that area.

I diverted their inquiring minds by commenting, "By the way, I read in the newspaper this morning that India is anxious for foreign travelers to visit and spend money here. I was happy to read this because we are sponsored by a man who appears on 200 television stations every week in America—and we will have a wonderful report to give him on our return. Also, my father is the head of a fellowship of businessmen with chapters all over the world. They will be excited to hear of how we have been treated in your country."

To lighten the atmosphere, I told the men, "I am a dairy farmer, and if you ever visit California, I want to give you a gallon of our ice cream."

Then I added, "We are not preaching, just telling our own personal stories of how Jesus loves us."

He thought for a moment, then replied, "Okay. If you just talk about Jesus, everything will be alright."

That night there were over 2,000 gathered for our outdoor meeting. What a joy to tell one story after another about my friend, Jesus—and how He offers hope and healing to men, women, and children, no matter where they live. I shared the account of the woman in the Bible who reached out to touch the hem of Jesus' garment and was instantly healed.

At the end of the rally, I offered a prayer that God would touch those who were sick. In the back of the crowd, a young girl was holding her mother's hand—and with the other she reached out for her healing. Suddenly, she began to scream in her language, "I can see! Momma, I can see!"

The entire village knew this blind girl—and witnessed the miracle as she received her sight.

Good news spreads fast, and the next night more than 8,000 jammed the same area. It was wonderful to talk about the power of God's Son.

Purely by coincidence, the communists had promoted a scheduled rally that same evening, with guest dignitaries from Moscow. They were expecting 10,000, but only a handful showed up. God's awesome power trumps politics!

Buddhist Monks

In nation after nation, Peru, Brazil, France, Greece, Kenya, Tanzania, Japan, and more, we were privileged to see thousands of lives transformed.

In Rangoon, Burma (now the Republic of Myanmar), the head priest of a Buddhist temple heard we were coming to his city and wanted to give his followers a special gift. So he invited the Abundant Life Youth Team to hold meetings in the temple. This was a first for us!

He was especially fascinated by the fact that we believed God heals today, and asked us to pray for those in the temple. It was amazing to see dozens of Buddhist monks with their shaved heads and orange wraparound robes, receiving our messages.

After Hong Kong and Hiroshima, Japan, the final stop was Honolulu, and we were both more than anxious to see our girls. It had been a tremendous sacrifice to be separated from them for so long. Just before flying to Los Angeles, we were excited to call the house and let the girls know we were on our way. When little Denice commented, "Daddy, I can't really remember what you look like," my heart fluttered. I knew it was time to be home.

A Hurting World

I have to be honest and admit, that on returning it was tough shifting gears from speaking on the average of three times a day through interpreters to making sure the cows were producing quality milk. But business was business, and I could not shirk my responsibilities.

Yet, what I had experienced in our travels was now part of my life and it could not be ignored. Practically every waking moment, whether I was overseeing the drive-in dairy stores or involved in the development of family enterprises, I couldn't erase the faces of a hurting world.

There was also a dire spiritual need here at home. So in the early 1960s I devoted 30 days to reaching the young people of California. At the invitation of various ministerial associations, we held a series of youth-oriented banquets that were extremely well received.

In San Diego, we booked a hotel banquet hall that seated 600. But when the designated evening came around and I arrived at the venue, a young man whom I had hired to help me with the details, came running toward me. He grabbed me by the collar and, stressed to the max, exclaimed, "Richard, you're in the biggest trouble of your whole life!"

"What are you talking about?" I wanted to know.

"You told me to set up for 600 people and there are twice that many already here! What in the world are we going to do?"

I smiled, put my hands on his shoulders, and reassuringly said, "Calm down. This is great news. God has answered our prayers."

We were able to feed the enthusiastic young people in two shifts—and they all stayed to enjoy the music and absorb the message that followed. It was a tremendous outreach.

My Dilemma

The Shakarian family would soon come to an important crossroads. The Fellowship launched by my father was now multiplying much faster then our herd of cattle. New chapters were being added by the hundreds, not just in the United States, but in scores of foreign nations. Thousands were attending international conventions.

The pressure on dad's time was enormous, as were the demands of the dairy. My dilemma was fast approaching his. Phone calls were coming in from every direction, "Richard, I know you are busy, but when can you come to our city?"

God was at work, and what He had in store was far greater than I ever imagined.

German Chancellor Willie Brandt

With Maasai tribe in East Africa

Conversing with Bhuddist Monks in Burma

Chapter 6

The Master's Plan

I'm not sure whether Reliance Dairy had outgrown Downey, or Downey had outgrown the farm, but one thing was clear. Houses were popping up everywhere—crowding out the cows!

In early 1960s our real estate holdings were becoming extremely valuable and the three generations of Shakarians, Isaac, Demos, and me, decided it was time to relocate.

We found the ideal spot. Eight hundred acres just off Highway 99 near Delano, California, in the San Joaquin valley about 30 miles north of Bakersfield.

Although I was still running the drive-in dairy stores in Southern California, I became excited about developing the new enterprise in Delano.

I was practicing the art of multi-tasking long before the term became popular—and I knew what it meant.

Opportunities were springing up everywhere, and I certainly didn't hesitate when an invitation came to join an expedition to search for Noah's Ark on 16,854-foot Mount Ararat. After all, I would be returning to the land of my heritage. It was late summer, 1962.

My only hesitation was the fact that Vangie had just lost her beloved sister, Naomi, in an automobile accident, but I felt this trip was a once-in-a-lifetime opportunity.

Those invited included highly-trained professional mountain climbers and researchers from various countries who had carefully studied the findings of previous explorations. On the way, we spent time in Paris with French explorer Fernando Navarro, who claimed to have discovered wooden timbers in a glacial crevasse on the mountain seven years earlier. The Bible specifically states that after the great flood, the ark rested "on the mountains of Ararat" (Genesis 8:4).

I had been on a strenuous exercise program, ready to brave the 16,000 foot mountain located in what is now Turkey, near the Russian border. At its peak there are 30 square miles of ice that never melts.

View from the Top

We flew into Istanbul, then to Erzurum, Turkey. From there we bounced along in an open truck. This was during the height of the Cold War, and in one village, I looked behind a gate next to a storefront and there sat a U.S. Pershing missile. The border was tense and on high alert, patrolled by Turks on one side and Russians on the other.

At the foot of the mountain the ten of us packed our bags onto mules—which often climbed faster than I could!

We encountered a Kurdish settlement at about the 8,000

foot level—where the inhabitants were dressed in vibrant colored clothing. These are a fierce people, yet very hospitable to visitors. We were cordially invited into a tent and served tea. They drank it just like my grandfather—with a sugar cube clenched between their teeth.

Then they brought out soup made from sour milk. I just knew it would be awful, so I generously passed the bowl on to a teammate!

When we reached our 11,000-foot base camp, I arose early on Sunday morning. It was a crisp, clear day, and from my vantage point I could see a vista of hundreds of miles—Turkey, Soviet-controlled Armenia, Russia, and Iran. It suddenly struck me that in every direction I looked there was religious repression. Men and women of all cultures were not free to worship as they pleased.

That morning, my tears would not stop flowing as I prayed for God to change the situation in this land that had meant so much to my family. That experience alone was worth every day of preparation and each difficult step I climbed.

Prior to our departure we had been warned to be on the lookout for volcanic boulders that work their way through the icy surface and come barreling down like cannon balls.

After one strenuous high climb, I was so tired that I announced to the team, "I can't go another step," and flopped down on the ice. About that time I heard a rumbling noise that grew increasingly louder. A rock was headed straight for me. I scrambled to my feet and quickly moved about six feet before the boulder hit right where I had been laying.

It was a huge disappointment when the snows moved in and, unfortunately, we were unable to reach the icy crevasse spotted by explorer Navarro.

On our descent, when we finally reached a grassy area, we spotted a wolf-dog close on our heels. I'm sure he thought he'd found his lunch! These are vicious creatures that can snap the neck of a large animal with one bite. I began noisily swinging my camera around until he skulked off.

When I returned to sunny Southern California, I couldn't erase the suppressed people of communist-controlled Armenia from my mind. I knew that someday, somehow, I would return and openly share the message that was burning in my heart.

Professional Advice?

As businessmen, our family invested heavily in prize bulls which we used for artificial insemination to increase the quality of our cows. The production of our dairy herd escalated to the point that each heifer was producing a full gallon of milk above average. This continued in the animals generation after generation.

I often accompanied my dad to cattle auctions, and once asked him, "How do you pick the bull you are going to buy?"

He found it difficult to explain, except to say, "One will stand out to me, as if there is a light shining over him. That's the one I choose."

After many years in the business, the manager of a

nationally-known breeding farm said, "Demos, you have been so good at selecting bulls. Do you receive any professional advice?"

"As a matter of fact, I do," my dad replied.

"Is this person in the business?" he wanted to know.

"Absolutely. He has cattle on a thousand hills."

"Well," said the dairyman, "Do you think I could meet him?"

This was my dad's golden opportunity. "I'll be more than happy to introduce Him to you. He's my Advisor and Friend, and His name is Jesus!"

Guidance from Above

The bulls and their offspring were like extended family to me. We raised the young cattle on a farm we owned near Modesto, California. We had about 1,000 heifers and I knew the lineage of every one—and could tell you from horseback who sired them.

Yes, I was in business, but again and again, God let me know that He was watching over and protecting me. For example, one weekend I took some of our managers pheasant hunting at our ranch in Northern California. There were six of us in the car. At one point, just as we were about to enter a ramp onto the freeway, Dave, who was driving, decided to step on the accelerator, even though it was a blind curve.

Suddenly, not knowing why, I screamed, "Stop!"

Just as we did, a huge truck carrying the biggest boulders

I had ever seen ran a stop sign and passed within inches of our car.

I realized on more than one occasion that God was guiding my steps.

THE MISSING BULL

On our farm, we were using only our top bulls for artificial insemination, the others for veal. So, as a member of Rotary International, I came up with the idea that we could donate some of our young bulls to other nations to raise their milk production. Rotary agreed to pay the shipping costs, and we began sending bulls to agricultural colleges in Japan, Israel, Central America, and elsewhere.

After sending a bull to a university in Mexico, we were invited down for a celebration. While there, I learned that the brother of the mayor owned a cattle operation.

Not long after returning home, it came to my attention that there had been a riot in the town and the prized bull was missing.

I knew the animal had to be somewhere. Then one day, as I was walking across the dairy, I suddenly had a revelation as to what had happened. So I called a local reporter who was Hispanic and told him, "I have a hot tip for you. It's about a bull we donated to Mexico."

Then I explained that during the riot the brother of the mayor protected the bull by taking it to his ranch. "I want you to write a story thanking him for saving the animal. He is a real hero!"

The article was written and a copy was sent to the newspaper in Mexico. A few days later the missing bull miraculously appeared at the university!

The Unthinkable

As the development for the new dairy in Delano was underway, the unthinkable happened. In 1964, my beloved grandad, Isaac—the patriarch of the Shakarian family, went to his heavenly reward. Because of his kind nature and wisdom, he was greatly loved. His funeral was one of the largest the city of Downey had ever seen.

As you can imagine, this created tremendous uncertainty for our future. My dad's commitment to the Fellowship was taking more and more of his time—with chapters being added all over the world. My own schedule was also under pressure. Yet, we focused like a beam of light on fulfilling the final dream of Isaac, a state-of-the-art dairy in Delano.

It was more than a farm, it was an agricultural showplace. The property was impressive—with a loft that was the biggest auditorium in town.

On opening day we had guided tours on wagons, pony rides, and free hot dogs for all. Over 10,000 people showed up to celebrate.

An Astounding Response

With the passing of Isaac, the siblings decided it would be best to sell the dairies, pay the estate taxes, and move on with life—and that's what happened.

Dad was still an active businessman, but now he was into shopping centers, oil exploration, and other enterprises. Best of all, he could devote much more of his time to the Fellowship, which was having tremendous growth worldwide.

With the drive-in dairies sold, I split my time between real estate development and major youth crusades across the nation.

I wanted to reach everyone, and especially high school and college students.

In San Bernardino, we rented the fairgrounds arena that seated 7,000. Instead of ministers, we invited gospel singer Andre Crouch and former gang member Nicky Cruz as our guest headliners.

I offered free reserved seating by ticket only to every kind of youth group in the city.

Just before the meeting started, a Baptist minister came running up to me, saying, "Mr. Shakarian, I have 28 people with reserved seating, but they are out of space."

He handed me his ticket. I looked at it and replied, "Sir, it says this is good until 7:15. That was a few minutes ago, but if you take your group to the balcony I know they will enjoy the program."

When I gave the altar call, over 700 people came to the front to give their lives to the Lord.

After the meeting we went to a local restaurant for a bite to eat, and the same Baptist minister was there. He quickly came over to our table, very excited. "Mr. Shakarian," he said, "I preach about salvation all the time, but tonight my mother went forward, and my niece climbed over the rail to get to the front. So I rushed down to pray with them. It was wonderful!"

In Portland, Oregon, 16,000 packed the building and another 2,000 could not get inside because the fire marshal wouldn't allow it. That evening Pat Boone was one of the featured guests.

My invitation to accept Christ lasted only two minutes, yet over 3,000 responded. Entire families came forward. In one group, 80 from a busload of 87 gave their hearts to the Lord.

I called several young people to the stage to relate what they had experienced. Five young girls stood there weeping, and I asked them, "Tell me what happened?"

"We are sisters," they said, "We came from the orphanage and tonight asked Jesus into our hearts."

I knew they would never be lonely again.

THE HEART OF CHICAGO

During the unrest of the Vietnam era of the late 1960s, I felt compelled to hold an event in Chicago, but the cost for arenas and auditoriums was exorbitant.

While driving around the city, desperately trying to find a suitable location, I spotted the huge Daley Plaza, an outdoor area in the heart of Chicago where major events are held.

Since it was out of the question to have seating, I named the rally "Stand Up For Jesus" and sent flyers to every church within 30 miles. By the start of the Wednesday lunchtime event, the Plaza was filling up fast. We had erected a small platform and rented the most powerful public address system available.

At the stroke of noon, I turned to our special music guest, Andre Crouch, and whispered, "Hit the most up-tempo song you have!"

Suddenly, people came swarming in from the adjacent government and office buildings. They had no idea what was going on, but they loved what they were hearing.

At one point that afternoon I told the crowd, "Today, we are going to dedicate this city to the Lord. Wherever you are, reach out and take the hand of the person next to you and bow your head as we pray."

Stoic middle-aged executives in suits were holding hands with fellow workers, secretaries reached for the hands of others. It was a powerful moment!

OIL BOOM AND BUST

As a young man, my dad learned much about the oil business, especially in locating potential successful drilling sites.

Using his knowledge, he traveled to Texas and discovered what turned out to be a great oil find and drew out the field. However, as they began drilling, just after hitting a big gusher, the banks came in and took over the operation. My father had no idea that the main partner was in serious financial trouble and the creditors seized the drilling rights.

Even though my father had found the field, he had nothing in writing. He had trusted the man and now dad was devastated.

Later, a geologist arrived at my father's home and said, "Mr. Shakarian, I represent a major oil company and have some papers I would like to show you." He pulled out my dad's original map of the Texas oil field.

"Is this your map?" he wanted to know. "Did you draw it?"

The field was now producing millions of dollars in oil and the man offered a proposal. "Would you be willing to come and work for us? We will pay you any amount you want."

It was an unexpected and generous offer, yet the work of the Fellowship was far more important to my father.

However, dad and I worked on some of the shallower oil fields in Texas and Oklahoma and he taught me everything he knew. Eventually, I decided to go into the oil business on my own.

With investor capital, I began searching for sites in Oklahoma. Others gave their opinions, but with the skills I had learned, I insisted, "No. Let's drill here—and we hit every strata."

Oil and gas was flowing, and we were reaping a harvest.

Gunshots in Oklahoma!

Once, after buying oil rights to a property, we were walking the land when suddenly my nephew, Kirk Glover, and I came upon a marijuana patch. About the same time, I heard gunshots.

When we headed back to our truck, we noticed that all four tires had been shot out. Then we saw the sheriff coming up the farm road. Following him were several cars filled with men with guns.

We were in trouble until I told the sheriff, "Sir, I own the oil rights to this property and I guess I'll have to call our attorney"—who was the son of a state senator and the nephew of the district attorney. The word must have spread to the marijuana growers because it was the end of our troubles.

My dreams, however, were soon shattered with the economic crash underway in 1986. The oil business hit the skids and banks were going under. It was horrendous. Back in California, I didn't know where to turn. Two more beautiful daughters had been added to our household, Brenda and Suzanne, and I was under tremendous financial pressure.

For the first time in my life, I felt fear, failure, and humiliation. It seemed as though I had failed God and my life was breaking apart.

"Code Blue!"

One morning, as I began dictating letters to my secretary, I suddenly felt a dull pain down my left arm and became disoriented. I said, "I think I need to lay down."

When Vangie learned of this, she immediately took me

to the hospital. While they were trying to get my blood pressure under control, the cardiologist, Dr. Anil Shah, made the decision to schedule an angiogram the next day.

During the procedure, Vangie heard the words, "Code Blue!" I had suffered an adverse reaction to the angiogram.

Immediately, Vangie left the waiting room—which was filled with people who had come to pray and offer support—and headed toward the area where she thought I was. My mother and father were following right behind her.

A nurse came flying out of my room and exclaimed, "It was serious—but now he is talking."

My father began to sob and his body shook uncontrollably.

When I woke up the Blue Team was standing over me. "Dr. Shah asked, "Did you feel me sock you?" I wasn't aware of a thing. He proceeded to explain, "I had to sock you three times on your chest—very hard."

Open heart surgery was planned for the next day. Thankfully, I did not have a heart attack, but every symptom indicated I was certainly leading up to one.

During the operation, Vangie kept telling those around her, "I have great peace. I know that God is not through with Richard, He has much more for him to do."

My time of recuperation brought me into a new and deeper relationship with the Lord.

THE SEVEN PILLARS

Several months later my wife and I were scheduled for a business appointment in Los Angeles. My doctor pleaded with me: "Richard, you cannot go. You're not strong enough to handle the stress."

We solved the problem by having a close friend, Bob, accompany Vangie and represent me—while I would relax in the lobby of the nearby Biltmore Hotel.

Seated in an oversized blue chair reading a book, suddenly there was a flash of light. It was so unusual I got up and went to the window to see what could have caused it, but there was no source of the light. Everything seemed okay, so I returned to the chair and suddenly the Lord began to speak to my heart. "There is something about Myself I am going to reveal to mankind. My pillars of truth."

My initial reaction was, "Lord, why are You talking to me?" At that point I felt as though I was the last person in line to receive such a divine word.

Then I saw what I can only describe as a vision, with seven pillars coming down from heaven. My eyes were wide open as what seemed like a giant scroll unfolded before me.

The first six pillars dealt with salvation, the outpouring of the Holy Spirit, healing and deliverance, the return of Israel, the goodness of God, and how spiritual gifts and callings would rest on ordinary people.

Then the scene changed and I found myself in heaven looking over the shoulders of angels as they were working on the seventh pillar—which descended and rested in the center, covering all mankind. It made a grand entrance with fire and smoke!

In this vision, I was suddenly transported back to earth, watching this magnificent pillar come toward God's people, who were milling around their own pillars of truth in a large courtyard that looked much like an ancient temple. The smoke dissipated and what appeared was a translucent roof with a radiant light that connected all the pillars and covered His people.

The light was exceedingly bright in the courtyard, but on the outside there was utter darkness. Those who were in the pitch black world could not see one another; their attention was riveted toward the light.

For the first time, all of God's people were under one covering. The light filled the entire area. It was as if billions of fine particles of God's glory rested on His people.

Inside rested His blessing and protection. Outside were the evil rulers of the world. Yet the light and fire were reaching out to mankind.

As the vision concluded, men and women were no longer running from pillar to pillar, divided by doctrines, but were united by the revelation of Jehovah's awesome power and His radiant light. It was a glorious picture of God's love and protection over His people.

I saw an army of believers being raised up, illuminating the darkness, bringing healing, and transforming lives.

When Vangie and Bob returned from their business meeting, they were concerned about me because they had been gone so long, not realizing I was having a marvelous visitation.

Vangie asked, "Are you all right?"

I responded with a smile, "Something very special happened—I'll tell you about it later."

A Lesson in Obedience

During this time I had started a Saturday morning

chapter at the international headquarters of the Fellowship and we televised the meetings into many cities of America.

I had been invited to attend a Fellowship retreat in Redlands, California, but on this particular Saturday I had been delayed, and wasn't sure about even going. During dinner, Vangie asked, "Do you feel like you should be there?"

"Yes, I feel I should go," so she encouraged me to make the trip.

When I arrived in Redlands on Saturday, the men were eating dinner and I quickly found out there were no more rooms available at the conference center. So I slept on a mat on the gym floor.

The next morning, I was seated on the platform enjoying the meeting, when an Italian pastor who was speaking, suddenly turned around, pointed at me, and spoke these unexpected words from the Lord:

"Oh Brother Shakarian, saith God unto thee, I have ordained thee that thou shall follow in the steps of thy father. Thou shalt move in leadership in this organization. Thou shalt be as Solomon. Thou shalt follow the steps of thy father, in this ministry. For I have ordained thee, saith God. Thou are a unicorn in the making. I shall strengthen thee.

Fear not to take this position, saith God unto thee, for I have ordained that thou shalt move forward. I shall gather about thee a strong leadership, far stronger than thy father which has gone forth through the years. Thou shalt not fear.

Thou shalt move for I have strengthened thee in administration in multiplying investments of God. I will give you the blessings of Abraham, Isaac, and Jacob. Thou shalt be unmovable if thou fasteneth thy eyes upon Jehovah-Jirah, saith God."

Wow! This came as a total shock to me—and to those gathered. Several asked, "Do you know this man?"

I had never seen him before in my life. "You're the ones who invited him," I replied.

THE RIGHT PRICE

While we were having a final luncheon, an older gentleman approached me and said, "Richard, there's a man in Hemet, California, who wants to see you. His name is Carl. He owns some property and needs help selling it. He'd like you to come and look it over."

"Well, how did he hear about me?" I asked.

"Oh, he used to sell hay to your dad and grandfather."

The next week I drove to Hemet and met Carl—a spry German fellow in his 80s.

He owned a large parcel of land and had given part of it to a university. He had invested heavily in paving and utilities, and even built and sold a few homes on the property. But when the economy turned south, he found himself in trouble.

"Richard, I've been trying to sell these 14 acres for $800,000, but no luck. It's been on the market two years. Can you sell it?"

"Yes," I quickly replied, "but you've given it the wrong price."

"Well, how much will it need to be lowered?" he wanted to know.

"Carl, you don't understand," I told him. "This is going to be a major intersection, and with the college and housing nearby, I wouldn't sell it for a penny under $1 million."

Wide-eyed, he promised, "Richard, if you can do that, I'll give you $100,000 over your regular commission." Then he added, "There's only one condition. When it goes into escrow, you have to close it the same week."

That was fair enough and I agreed.

As I drove away, I began praying, "Lord, please send me a buyer."

Within two weeks I spoke with some Chinese men who had an investor who owned an eyeglass factory in Taiwan. They weren't Christians or part of my circle of friends. I brought them to see the property and they immediately wanted to purchase it. We went to Chicago Title in San Bernardino on Monday and they put up a cashiers check for $100,000.

On Tuesday I was on the other side of Los Angeles when I received a frantic call from Carl. He said, "I'm here at the escrow office. Come and help me. These Chinese men are trying to play games."

When I arrived, the buyers were trying to lower the price and had asked for an extra three days. So, in the conference room I told them, "I'll make you a better offer. Take all of your cash back and we'll let you out of the deal."

On Friday, the Chinese men promptly showed up with

a $900,000 cashiers check and closed on the property.

A few days later, Carl wrote me a personal check for $100,000—plus the commission. All on a handshake. God is good!

Because I was obedient to the voice of the Lord, He led me to a great blessing which was so needed at the time.

Saving the Deal

On the heels of that transaction, I received a call from a friend who had put together about 20 separate pieces of property near Palm Springs. He had a grand real estate strategy, but was fast reaching the end of his rope because he couldn't come up with the taxes and mortgage payments to hold it together.

After no serious bids, he let his agent go and asked me to help him sell the acreage. The asking price had been just over $8 million and I raised it to $12 million because of recent infrastructure improvements by the government. The clock was ticking and if he didn't sell, he'd have to break up the large parcel.

A few days later, a Chinese woman who was a partner and a person I used as a translator, brought an Asian investor to my office. I learned to drink lots of tea!

After agreeing on a deal, the man missed an escrow payment and I quicky figured out that he was stalling until the owner would be at the brink of total collapse.

Even though my partner kept vouching for the investor, I wanted nothing to do with him. So I cancelled the transaction. He was not a happy camper!

I had no other buyer in mind, but I trusted the Lord to bring the perfect prospect to me.

Within two weeks another interested party appeared and I told him the unvarnished truth: "If you don't make some kind of payment, the seller will lose the property. It will no longer be one parcel."

The man pulled out his checkbook and on the spot wrote out a check for $500,000 and handed it to the seller. This was outside of escrow and the sale was saved.

Isaac, Richard, and Demos doing business

The state-of-the-art Reliance Dairy in Delano, California

Climbing Mount Ararat

16,000 at Portland Youth Rally

Striking oil in Oklahoma

Chapter 7

A Hunger for Freedom

It was a surprising request.

In early 1990, officials from the government of Armenia, flew to Los Angeles to promote opportunities in their nation —which was on the verge of independence from the Soviet Union.

They especially wanted to meet my father for lunch since the Shakarian name was well-known in the homeland, plus they were well aware that he headed a worldwide businessmen's organization—with contacts everywhere. Dad asked me to join them.

"Please, Mr. Shakarian, will you come to Armenia?" they pleaded. "We will take care of all the arrangements and help you any way we can." This was quite a request coming from a Soviet-dominated government.

Dad did not feel strong enough to make the trip, and asked if I would take his place. As I prayed about it, I realized God was opening a door and I should walk through it. So I decided to put my real estate business on hold and accept the invitation.

I asked, "What is the largest auditorium in the capital city?" They told me it was the sports arena and I requested that they book it for our visit there.

"Are you sure?" they wanted to know. "There are not enough Christians in the entire country to fill it." Yet, they agreed.

I also requested that they print 20,000 copies of the Gospel of John in Armenian—to be ready upon our arrival. Think of it! They would be printed on the Central Committee Communist press and be paid for by the Fellowship.

"Yes, we will do as you ask," they replied, treating it as a business deal.

Such permission was unheard of. Especially since Armenian Christians had been greatly persecuted dating back to the time of the genocide.

There were 10 in our group, including our daughter, Brenda, and our 10-month-old granddaughter, Brianna. We flew first to Moscow, then caught a plane to Yerevan, the capital city of Armenia.

A government official met us at the airport on a beautiful May afternoon where we were presented with a detailed daily schedule—we learned later that our host was a four-star KGB officer. Everything was paid for by the government, including local transportation, hotels, and meals.

We would be looking at economic opportunities and holding rallies every night in a different city. I really did not expect them to arrange so many meetings, but to the officials in charge, it was a trade-off worth risking.

The Prophecy of St. Gregory

From the moment we stepped foot on Armenian soil, we could feel the political tension. This was a time when the Soviet empire, under the leadership of Mikhail Gorbachev, was experiencing Glasnost and Perestroika—massive economic and political reforms.

Armenia had been annexed by the Soviet Union in 1922, but now there was a burning hunger for independence.

On our first day we were driven to a city about 40 miles from the capital. The area had suffered a major earthquake and we witnessed refugees living in metal shipping containers. Yet, these proud people, many who had lost limbs, had not lost their dignity.

On the road we stopped and talked with a film crew from Europe who were documenting the devastation. After our conversation they said, "Our next stop is a business meeting down the road." It was the event where we were scheduled to speak!

That evening, as several thousand jammed into a sports arena, we began singing "Hosanna"—a word that denotes God Almighty. At first only a few joined in worship. Then I noticed some of the older women began to raise their hands and lift their voices to God. Others caught the spirit and soon everyone in the arena was singing in unison. Remember, it had been decades since an event of this nature was allowed to take place in Armenia.

As part of my message, I related the prophecy of St. Gregory, who brought Christianity to Armenia 1,600 years earlier. God spoke through the prophet:

"I am the Lord, the only begotten Son of God. The first and the last, and there is none besides Me. Nay, My glory I will not give to another. Nor My praise to images of gold and silver. Behold, thou art a chosen vessel [King] Tiradtes, to carry My name to kings and nations. Yea, gird thyself for this holy mission. Make thy people the first Christian nation. Fear not, I have redeemed thee. Do not be dismayed, for I am with thee. With My right hand, I will uphold thee. Yea, assume thy task: lead the people to Me. Set the Gospel's torch on Ararat's lofty height, to illuminate the length and breath of the Orient. God Almighty is with thee. Hear His intent."

The ruling king of that time, Tiridates, not only embraced the message, but testified to being healed in body and mind by the power of God. He ordered all pagan temples to be demolished and together, he and St. Gregory brought Armenia to Christ.

Is it Real?

I shared with the audience, "This is being fulfilled today. Some of you will hear with your ears, but others will hear the inner voice in your heart." Then, as I concluded, I said, "Ladies, if you will excuse me, I want to speak to the men for a moment. The Word of God never dies. It is just as alive and effective today as it was 1,600 years ago. If you will be the one who will give his heart to Christ, I want you to quickly come to the front so I can pray with you."

I only uttered the invitation once—and over 800 men streamed forward. As I prayed, tears flowed down their cheeks. Soon, the women came and stood along side them.

As I looked over the scene, I saw men wearing the uniform of the Russian National Guard. They were there to help the earthquake victims, but to my amazement, these men responded just like the Armenians. Joining them were members of the Red Army. The butts of their rifles were resting on the floor, but their hands were raised to heaven, crying out to God.

Night after night, in city after city, the response was the same. And when we prayed for those who needed healing, the testimonies were miraculous.

An Unexpected Night

After a week of daytime appointments with government agencies and nightly meetings, we were all exhausted.

On what was to be an "off" night, Vangie and some of the women were invited to attend an event featuring the Armenian National Dance troupe.

For me, however, one more meeting had been arranged at an outdoor stadium in another city.

Over the years, I had been privileged to be in some of the most anointed services you can imagine, but I wasn't quite prepared for what was about to take place.

It was a picturesque evening, with the stadium lined with eucalyptus trees and flags. Right behind the crowd rested the snow-capped Mount Ararat.

I felt impressed to speak on the subject of God's healing

power and began by sharing the story of how the Almighty created the first man and woman in the Garden of Eden—which was located in that part of the world. Then I added, "In that beautiful place, in the cool of the evening, the Lord came down to walk and talk with them."

Just as I said those words, a wind began to blow. Flags were fluttering and the trees were rustling—it was as if God Almighty was making an entrance into the stadium.

Everywhere I looked, the eyes of the people were wide open, wondering, "What is going on?"

I continued by telling the story of the woman who reached out and touched the hem of Jesus' garment—and was made whole. "You can experience this too," I told the assembled crowd. "Regardless of your need, reach out and touch the Lord."

MIRACLE! MIRACLE!

Suddenly there was a commotion at the front of the stage. A man who was mute began to speak—and his family verified his healing. Through the interpreter, he exclaimed, "When you prayed, God picked me up in the air and threw me on the ground—and I began to speak."

In the stands, another person screamed, "Miracle, miracle!" A woman who had been lame for over 40 years was walking.

This continued for almost an hour. What was amazing was the fact that the healings were not occurring simultaneously. There was a delay between each one—as if Jesus Himself was walking through the crowd, stopping to touch one person, and then moving on to the next.

When I gave the invitation for people to receive Christ, hundreds came forward for prayer.

After the meeting concluded, I took a few moments to walk along the runner's track inside the stadium. I could hardly drink in what had taken place.

As I was returning to our group, a refined woman in a red business suit headed straight for me. She said, "Mr. Shakarian. I am an atheist. I have terrible arthritis, but while you were speaking, I was cured." She put her hands in the air, rejoicing.

"It wasn't me," I assured this jubilant woman. "It was the Lord."

"Do you now believe in God?" I asked. She looked at her pain-free hands and responded, "Yes! Yes, I do."

"Will you accept Jesus into your heart?"

I prayed with her and she was aglow with the Spirit of God.

"How Do You Do This?"

Our final meeting was in an impressive sports arena on a prominent hill in Yerevan. Starting early on that Sunday afternoon, people began making their way into the 15,000 seat venue. Soon it was completely jammed and the officials had to lock the doors.

The manager came on stage and whispered, "There are another 4,000 outside, but we have arranged for a loud speaker system so they can hear everything." There was no prior publicity to attract such a crowd, just word of mouth.

We tried to have a Gospel of John available for each person in attendance, but it was impossible. Sadly, we had run out of copies because everywhere we went people were hungry for the Word of God.

The message of the Cross did not fall on deaf ears or hardened hearts. In that one meeting, over 6,000 gave their lives to Christ.

That same day, there was political upheaval. The Soviets heard that the Armenians were going to topple the statue of Lenin in the city square.

After the meeting, we were invited to the home of some Christian Armenians who had prepared a meal. The team went to the home, but I was asked to accompany government officials to a dinner at a hotel.

During our meal, a man came in and was excitedly reporting how Armenian soldiers had been shot at the train station and Russian tanks were rolling on the streets. In the meantime, across the city, the group Vangie was with looked out of a window and could see a tank prominently positioned on a hill. Concerned, they ate quickly and headed back to the hotel, dodging armed, angry crowds.

It was almost midnight before our whole team met back at the hotel.

Even though it was very late, I received a message that I was to go to the home of our host. Accompanying me was Paul Toberty, one of our team members from Los Angeles. We walked over to the gentleman's apartment near the center of the city.

At his residence, our official host turned to me and asked, "Mr. Shakarian, how did you do this?"

"What do you mean?" I responded.

"Well, you had no advertising and there are only about 8,000 Christians in all of Armenia, yet you had thousands of people come to your meetings?"

I could tell he was under a lot of pressure because of the unexpected response we were receiving—not to mention the volatile uprising in the streets.

"Do you really want to know?" I asked him. "Yes," he said.

"Let me explain. If you starve the people for over 70 years and don't give them good food and nourishment, they become hungry. Then when people fly in from another country and offer them the best food possible—the Bread of Life—they receive it with joy."

The man dropped his head because he knew the truth of what I was saying. It was the desperate hunger for God in the hearts of men and women. Before we left, I am delighted to report that this KGB official prayed to receive the Lord as his Savior.

A Word, Specifically for Me

That same summer, the international convention of the Fellowship was held in Anaheim, California. One of the guest speakers was Ulf Ekman, a noted Swedish pastor and charismatic leader.

On the final night of the event, July 7, 1990, I was seated

on the platform of the packed auditorium when Ekman suddenly walked over, pointed his finger directly at me and began to speak under a powerful anointing:

> *"There have been several things that have been trying to pull you away. There have been people who said, 'You are only in this because of your father.' But you know your time...you know your calling. It has not yet been developed, but you know that you have been called with this man (pointing to my father, Demos).*
>
> *You have been called by the Spirit of God to carry that which your father was given from heaven, and the people who have been rejecting you, and attacking you, I will deal with them, says the Spirit of God. Because I do not see after the flesh.*
>
> *I say GO! Do what I've put into man's hearts! Be blessed and lift up your head, and do not let people put you down, because I have placed you in a position and I will strengthen you. And more revelation will come.*
>
> *And then, oh in the future. Oh, in the future for the second part of your calling. The crowds...the crowds...the crowds...and the teaching of My Word, says God."*

At this time, my activities with the Fellowship were to help my father any way I could. As a businessman, I was involved with real estate.

Yet, for the second time, I was given a specific prophecy concerning my future—the first at the retreat in Redlands, California. I knew God was speaking directly to me.

Changing the Atmosphere

That night, Ekman delivered a second prophecy. The subject matter amazed me, especially since I had just returned from Armenia, a neighboring country of Iran. Ekman said:

> *"Iran, Iran, Iran. Yes, you will plant your ministry in the nation of Iran. There will be supernatural doors into that nation and nations around yes Iraq and Syria. It's not just for Fellowships to be started, it's not just for chapters and the blessings...it's more than that.*
>
> *It is the shaking of the nations because, says the Spirit of God, the time is coming where I will shake the nations, I will shake them, yes you have heard it and you have heard it again says the Spirit of God.*
>
> *In my timetable says the Spirit of God, there is a time for lifting up and a time for breaking down, there is a time for stability and a time for shaking. Not just a few people, not just some small Fellowships, but the participation of the revival of that nation is on your shoulders and is part of the vision that God has called you to."*

Since hearing those words, I have eagerly watched how the Lord has begun to move in the Middle East.

On August 23, 1990, Armenia declared its independence, becoming the first non-Baltic republic to secede from the Soviet Union.

We believe God brought us to this land at this particular time for a divine purpose. Our visit to Armenia has been heralded as the spark which brought a spiritual awakening to the nation and literally changed the atmosphere. To God be the glory!

Here's the exciting news. Today, there are Spirit-led churches dotted all across Armenia—some with up to 20,000 members.

Armenia has an open border with Iran, and we are thrilled by the reports of how the life-changing message of Christ is reaching so many in this Persian nation.

16,000 in Armenia

Chapter 8

A New Day

I didn't know why, but in July 1992, I felt an overwhelming urge to have an extra-special birthday party for my father—his 79th. Vangie questioned, "Why this year? Don't you think we should wait until he is 80?"

"No," I responded, "I have the feeling we need to do something now."

About 300 invited guests attended the event, and after the customary shish-kabob dinner, we brought out a giant cake iced with the continents of the world. It was a memorable occasion.

At the time, dad's travel schedule had been significantly curtailed and he asked me to take over almost all of his speaking engagements and personally visit as many chapters of the Fellowship as possible.

On the road, there would be a nightly phone call, "Son, tell me what happened today"—and I would give my dad a detailed account of the meetings and the miraculous things God was doing. "Oh, that is wonderful," he would respond.

This was his life—and he savored every moment.

WHAT ARE YOU TRYING TO TELL ME?

There was an upcoming convention scheduled in Brighton, England, July, 1992. Again, dad asked, "Would you go and represent me?"

This was not the first time dad had asked for my help. Several years earlier, in 1984, he suffered an unexpected stroke, but had made a steady recovery and was able to speak at many of the conventions. Yet, he had to conserve his strength and carefully allocate his time.

The conference in Brighton ended on Saturday night, and around midnight, after most of the people had departed, the director of the Fellowship in France, Bruno Berthon, and his wife Chantel, approached me and said, "Richard, could we find a private place where we can pray?"

We found an empty ballroom and pulled up a few chairs. Then the wife of the director began to pray. Suddenly she began to speak prophetic words, including these:

> *"There will be great changes in the Fellowship. Don't be afraid, I am in control. I have a place for you; it is reserved for you. There is something inside you; it is different from your father. You will shine as a star, you will shine in a different way than your father. I will call your father back—I am in control.*
>
> *Don't panic, do not go out. You have not found your place yet. You will find your place; you will shine. When you find your place, all that I have put in you will come out. It will pour out like many waters.*

I see your feet with wings on them quickly traveling the whole world.

The rushing of the Holy Spirit by your feet. Beautiful are the feet of those who carry the gospel. Something about Me that is unknown, that you will bring to the world. All that is within you will come out."

I returned to my hotel room and was very troubled by the words, "I will call your father back"—I questioned, "Is my father going to die?"

My flight was early the next morning but I didn't get a minute's sleep.

When I arrived home from England, Vangie met me at the airport and I asked her to immediately drive me to see my dad.

A Written Document

During the early months of 1993, my father's physical condition was deteriorating. Plus, there were repeated rumors that a power-play was going on behind the scenes (with a few international directors) regarding who would lead the Fellowship if Demos were no longer here.

My father spent time with each of his top officers, asking them what they saw for the future of the Fellowship. What he heard caused him to be concerned about the spiritual well-being of the organization.

Following this, dad took me aside, and confided, "Richard, you have the anointing and are the only person who can hold the Fellowship together. So I have written a document naming you as the president should anything happen to me."

We reflected on the past and talked about how God had protected our family from the Armenian genocide, brought us to the shores of America and gave us a vision to reach the world.

This was a private conversation and the details of his wishes were not communicated to anyone else.

A Broken Heart

In May, 1993, about eight weeks before the international convention of the Fellowship, which was to be held in Boston, Massachusetts, to my father's great disappointment, he learned that the rumors of a plan to divide the Fellowship were true. Such news broke his heart.

It came as a shock the morning dad walked into the headquarters building and fired his executive officers—including the person who controlled the bank accounts. He had never done anything like this in his life, but, after months of prayer and soul-searching, he believed it was the only way to save the Fellowship.

Ready for Heaven

Dad flew with us to the Boston convention, and it seemed to all of us as if a breath of fresh air was flowing through the Fellowship.

When we returned to Los Angeles, we began making plans for his 80th birthday celebration. However, dad interjected, "I'm not sure about a big party. I really don't feel up to it."

A few days later he was rushed to the hospital with heart complications. Oral Roberts came to visit, but told the family privately that he believed, "Demos is getting ready for heaven." Dad had asked the Lord for 80 years and God honored his wishes.

My father spent his 80th birthday in a hospital bed, and two days later, with our family gathered at his bedside, there was a moment when we all joined in singing. The glory of God descended and I had never experienced anything quite like it. Peacefully and quietly, the patriarch of our family passed into the presence of his Maker to receive his eternal reward. At that moment it was as if every light in the room dimmed. He was gone.

I had lost my closest confidante and best friend. He was my encourager—always there for me. It was impossible to describe my loss.

His funeral in Downey was attended by leaders of the Fellowship who had flown in from many nations—plus there were scores of government, community, and agricultural officials who honored his life. It was a glorious memorial service.

Directions from Above

The following day a luncheon meeting was held that

included the international officers of the Fellowship. After the meal, the Fellowship attorney stood and announced to those present, "I would like to read a notarized document that Demos Shakarian wrote and signed six months ago."

The contents had never before been revealed, but it stated that it was his wish for me to become president of the Fellowship. I felt overwhelmed at the responsibility that had now been placed on my shoulders.

I knew the future would be in God's hands, so I said to those gathered, "Let's get down on our knees and pray. The Lord will show us the direction we must take."

While I was seeking God, the Holy Spirit spoke a clear word to my spirit, "You are to be the great encourager."

I realized that what it would take to enlarge the vision and impact the world was the simple gift of help and encouragement. The Lord would supply the rest of the gifts at their moment of need.

"This Is Mine!"

Following the luncheon, we went to the Fellowship headquarters building with the directors. It was there that the hearts of these men were revealed.

Five of the international directors said, "Richard, we need to talk with you alone, without any of the officers present."

What I heard in that conference room confirmed every warning given to my father.

These men had been appointed years before for the

purpose of expanding the work worldwide. But now, the five had devised a plan to divide up the world—with each totally controlling their territory.

They had built up strong loyalties to themselves in their nations and were ready to expand their authority even further. Evidently, these wealthy men thought they could buy the Fellowship. They didn't realize it was not for sale. The Fellowship belongs to God.

It was obvious that these individuals had long been planning for this moment. Ignoring the letter written by my father. The director who was in charge of Europe walked over to a large map of the world that was hanging on the wall and stated, "Richard, you can call yourself by any title you want, but these parts of the world are mine." Then, with his finger he drew a circle from England to Europe, Russia and North Africa. With a tone of defiance, he announced, "This is *mine!*"

The steel look in his eye and the inflection in his voice sent chills down my spine.

Another spoke up, "We do not want you to write to our people. We will communicate with them directly. You just stay in America and do whatever you want here."

I was stunned—especially since these gentlemen were in an appointed position and I had every right to rescind their involvement. But this was not the time, nor the place, for a confrontation. God would have to resolve the matter.

I did say, however, "I do believe members of the Fellowship would be interested in the events surrounding the passing of my father. And I plan to put it in writing."

They reluctantly agreed.

At the time of my dad's passing the organization had sizable debt and cash flow problems, which could partly be attributed to the lack of support from those who harbored other motives.

WHAT PATH SHOULD I TAKE?

During the last few months of my father's life, knowing that I may soon be taking the reins, there was one phrase he repeated to me again and again, "Richard, break the mold."

I had no idea what those words meant—nor did he. But a new day was dawning, and I prayed daily for God to show me the right path to take.

Instead of listening to the directive of those five men, we stood on the promise that "With God, nothing is impossible" (Luke 1:37).

I loved my father and wanted to honor his wishes, but more important, I wanted to honor my heavenly Father. So Vangie and I made the decision to travel to every part of the world—putting aside the negative, sharing the stories of the amazing things the Lord was doing, and preparing men and women for eternity.

I prayed, "Lord, I am placing everything in Your hands and know You will take care of any problems, I just want to share Your love."

I had no idea what the future held for the Fellowship, but I was soon to find out.

Demos' 79th birthday

Demos and Rose

Richard and Demos

With Oral Roberts

Chapter 9

The Confirmation

There was no turning back!

Yes, my appointment as President of the Fellowship was the desire of my earthly father, but it had been confirmed again and again by words of prophecy given to godly men and women.

In the natural, the situation looked bleak—especially with long-time leaders digging in their heels, wanting to exert whatever personal power they had. However, I was reminded of the words spoken by Mother Teresa: "If you judge people, you have no time to love them."

One night, during this soul-searching chapter of my life, the Lord clearly spoke to my spirit:

> *"Richard, I am the One who chose you to replace your father, I have begun a new time for the Fellowship and will blow into it a new breath of life. I am purifying it by raising up new, responsible leaders. Richard, I will help you make the right choices and choose men to work in unity.*

No one can stand against Me. I oppose the proud and give grace to the humble. Be confident, be patient. At the right time, I will do new things. I do not want a human work. I will make men know My ways."

Everything rested in God's hands.

To let the world know what was taking place, I began sending cassette tapes to our International Directors and chapter leaders (CD's would be added a little later). They contained uplifting stories of how God was changing lives and how the original vision was being fulfilled. I was also sending updates by letter.

It was not until Vangie and I made a fact-finding trip to Europe that I realized the impact of our communication.

More than Encouragement

A snowstorm welcomed us when we landed at the airport in Paris. We intentionally booked into the Grand Hotel near the Opera House—the same place my father stayed the last time he visited France.

After settling in, I began to phone several of our leaders in the region, inviting them to a dinner at the hotel. I had no idea what kind of reception I would receive, but in one call after another the people sounded excited that we were there.

During the meal and the question-answer session which followed, I asked, "How many are receiving our cassettes and letters?" Nearly everyone—and they encouraged me to continue the reports.

I was especially thrilled that these leaders decided to organize a group to attend the upcoming International Convention in Anaheim, California.

It was a spiritual adrenaline boost when one man exclaimed, "I played your last cassette six times! It really ministered to me!"

A Surprise Guest

Our next destination wasn't on the original schedule, but we flew to London. After arriving at the Intercontinental Hotel, I began to contact some of the Fellowship leaders I knew in that part of England. At a hastily-arranged dinner, one man spoke up, "I know you're looking forward to the regional convention of the Fellowship this weekend in Blackpool."

This was news to me. I knew absolutely nothing about it! The event had been arranged by the same gentleman who, several months earlier, stood before a map at our headquarters in California, drawing a circle around Europe, saying, "This is *mine!*"

The people at our London dinner made all the arrangements for us to travel to Blackpool, and when we walked into the convention, those attending were not only surprised—they welcomed us with open arms. That is, everyone but a few of the leaders in charge. All they could say from the platform was, "We are glad to have a young man and his wife here from California." But the people knew I was the International President.

Our purpose in being there was not to embarrass the director, but to help unite the Fellowship.

When it was time for us to leave, hundreds stood in line to shake our hands and thank us for coming. The dissident leader reluctantly admitted, "Richard, they really love you."

An Unexpected Word

In early May, 1994, Vangie and I attended a regional convention of the Fellowship in Sweden. While there, we learned that Ulf Ekman would be holding special services in Moscow.

Ekman is the same man who gave the prophecy at our Anaheim, California international convention mentioned earlier. We felt the need to go—just to sit under the teaching ministry of this anointed servant of God.

The venue was at a KGB headquarters building at what seemed like the last local train stop in a suburb of Moscow.

We arrived without any advance notice—and just wanted to receive whatever the Lord had in store. We were seated about halfway back in the auditorium, enjoying the meeting, when suddenly, Ekman spotted us and we were called to the platform.

The minute our feet stepped on the stage, Ulf Ekman, turned our direction and gave an unexpected prophetic word, which was recorded. In a firm, forceful voice, he said:

"Thus says the Spirit of the Lord. You did not come here by coincidence nor accident. You came here because of a thirst and a need. And you came here in preparation for the future. For I, according to My Word, have thrust you into that which I have called you to. Yes, I've set you there. I separated you even before you were born to carry on the work of your father, only in a different measure and a different way, than both him and you understand or think.

So I speak to you tonight. Do not be afraid. Do not be dismayed. Be bold and courageous for I am with you, says the Lord. I am with you more than you are willing to believe. So this very night, I remove rejection. I render you totally insensitive to what man is thinking about you.

For what I root and what I plant, I keep and I guard. I will let My servant stand. Other people say, will he fall? Will he be able to accomplish, or will he fail? Right now fear of failure is going. Right now I put a steel bar in your spinal cord, and you will become insensitive to the thoughts and the schemes of man, it will not bother you. I'm with you, says the Lord. I am with you.

Oh, there will be changes. There will be new directions. But there is a mantle, a mandate, a calling and anointing for a new time, new ways, new peoples, new waves. Oh, just wait and the wave will come. It will lift you. It will carry you into your destiny. When it is fulfilled you will laugh and rejoice. You will lead with strength and an easiness—an anointing to lead. Those enemies, like dry leaves that fall on the ground, will amount to nothing. Those that rebelled, the earth swallowed them. Again, people will be swallowed up. You'll not hear them. You'll not see them. They will not bother you. They are gone.

You will have the wisdom of the anointing of the Holy Spirit, the discernment, not just in catastrophes, but in the daily work. Oh your heart is bubbling over. As I put a steel bar in your spine, I also put a guard by your heart to discern the motives of man and the limitations of your ministry and the fulfillment of My plan. Be anointed, says the spirit of God."

Vangie and I struggled to contain the emotions we both felt. Our hearts were overflowing. Without question, the Lord led us to Moscow to hear from heaven. It was a confirmation that we were in the perfect center of God's will.

After the meeting Ekman told us, "The Lord has been dealing with me all day about you, and I believe your being here is ordained of the Lord."

From that moment forward, we could see God's hand at work. Those who had personal agendas eventually fell by the wayside and were replaced by men with a true vision.

Over the years, the Spirit of God has led me to appoint scores of individuals to leadership—men who have a fire and passion to expand the Kingdom, regardless of the cost.

Giovanni's Encounter

Today, as we will detail in the next chapters, the Fellowship is making its mark on cultures and transforming nations. However, this movement has never been fixated on numbers, our focus has always been on changing one heart at a time.

Permit me to give you an example. Several years ago, during the unrest that followed the Vietnam era, we decided to conduct an outreach in Rome—taking about 100 people with us. Each night there were large banquets where local businessmen and government officials were extended invitations to be our guests. They would hear the inspiring stories of men whose lives had been changed by a personal relationship with Christ.

A friend from Southern California, John McTernan, had moved to Rome. He formerly owned a car dealership, but felt led to buy a factory in Italy and build a church.

One problem: he didn't speak Italian! So he went to the University of Rome in search of a tutor. This is where he met Giovanni, the head of the Communist Student Union.

At the time, the Italian government was in a state of flux. He told me, "At the university, there are Marxist slogans painted on the walls and broken windows as a result of riots. But Giovanni agreed to teach me Italian—and he's doing a good job."

John invited Giovanni to have lunch with us at the beautiful Excelsior Hotel, and I invited him to the upcoming banquet as our guest.

When Giovanni heard that five ministers of the government including the minister of education would be in attendance, he eagerly accepted. We learned that he had been wanting to talk with the official for many months and this might be his chance. Giovanni then asked, "Would it be possible for me to bring along some members of our student cabinet?"

After John agreed, he said, "I have only one request. That I will be able to ask questions."

"No problem," he was told.

FROM MARX TO THE MASTER

The Hilton hotel ballroom was jammed, and I'm sure some of the student leaders had never been to such a fancy place. After the meal we broke into a smaller room for those who had questions.

One of the student cabinet guests immediately spoke up, "You men are nothing like I expected. There is no confrontation."

He obviously had a pre-conceived notion that we were masters of the capitalist system and stooges who were there to promote some economic plan.

I assured him, "We have only one Master, the Lord Jesus Christ. There is no financial or other motive involved. We just want to demonstrate the power of the love of God."

This was a whole new world for Giovanni. Before we

arrived, when John and he discussed spiritual matters, he told the Marxist leader, "You are not honest, because you do not know what Jesus said,"—and he challenged him (as an intellectual exercise) to translate the Gospels from Italian into English.

When we arrived, he had already translated Matthew, Mark, and Luke. On learning this, I said, "Giovanni, if you really want to know about Jesus, my favorite book in the Bible is St. John. You will not only learn about Jesus, but about yourself."

Soon after, Giovanni accepted Christ as his Master and Lord—and eventually became the pastor of the large church built by my friend, John.

Just as one seed can produce an abundant harvest, miracles multiply because of one transformed life.

CHAPTER 10

OPENING PALACE DOORS

I have been asked again and again, "Richard, why is the Fellowship growing at such an unprecedented pace and being embraced by the leaders of nations everywhere?"

To me, the answer is simple. First, we are not a church or a denomination—just business people with a passion to see God at work in the lives of men and women.

The relationships we have made with presidents and prime ministers cross all lines of politics, religion, race, or language. In God's sight, all human hearts are the same.

In country after country, many of the leaders in the Fellowship hold high positions in medicine, education, commerce, law, and government. As a result, we are warmly received by the highest officials in the land, in their offices, palaces, and presidential homes.

A Leader in Turmoil

On a trip to the beautiful country of Austria, one of our men arranged for us to meet with Kurt Waldheim. I had followed his career for years when he was in the headlines during his ten year term as Secretary General of the United Nations and being president of Austria.

His elegant apartment, overlooking the Opera House and the historic city of Vienna, had been one of the homes of the last Emperor of the nation.

He and his wife, Madam Elizabeth, gave Vangie, me, and our friend, a very warm welcome. However, at the time, Waldheim was under tremendous political pressure from some in the Jewish community because of accusations that he was once a Nazi. Waldheim, who was a Catholic, told us it was nothing more than accepting a communications job at the age of 18 with no political agenda. He felt hurt by the accusations.

He had heard about our Fellowship and wanted to learn more. I explained, "We encourage business people to rise to their full potential, redirecting their energies and aligning themselves with God so they can grow spiritually as well as financially."

At the conclusion of a rather lengthy conversation, I asked if I could pray with him. He immediately stood to his feet and we all held hands as I asked the Lord to guide him in his current situation.

IGNORING THE BOMBS

Jerusalem has always been a favorite destination—not only because of what took place there 2,000 years ago, but for its spiritual and political significance today.

In 2004, while guests of the government and staying at the David Citadel Hotel, I received word that Prime Minister Ariel Sharon would like to meet with me and two other Christian leaders from the West who were also visiting Israel. This took place two years before he suffered his devastating stroke.

However, the morning of the scheduled visit, there was a horrific suicide bus bombing in the city—after a relatively violent-free period.

Because of this brutal act of terrorism, I thought the appointment would be cancelled, but it was not.

After going through extremely tight security, we entered the conference room adjoining the presidential office and were greeted by Sharon and eight of his top aides. The three of us were seated directly across from this renown leader.

Sharon began by talking about the bombing—then continued for an hour and a half, discussing the situation in Israel.

Why did he spend so much time with the three of us? We represented millions of people and he knew his words would be amplified worldwide.

At one point Prime Minister Sharon stated, "The reason I did not cancel this meeting is because no act of violence should be able to alter the course of events."

From his heart, he shared his desire for peace, but how this required a partner.

He singled out Iran in particular as using Hezbollah and Hamas to ferment violence. It took many years for the West to acknowledge what Sharon was telling us that day. Everybody knew, but somehow the great nations shielded their eyes and refused to take action.

I was amazed at the patience and temperance of this man, being a former general.

When it was my time to speak, I shared from my heart how only a relationship with God can change lives and bring true peace.

A Staff from Moses

On this trip we met with the archaeologists who were excavating King David's palace grounds just outside the old wall of Jerusalem. Our official guide, whose name was Moses, asked me, "Is there anything we can do for you?"

I thought for a moment and commented, "I really love to read the inspiring psalms written by King David. It would be such a treat to have lunch on these grounds, eating the same kind of food he would have enjoyed."

The next day there was a canopy erected, and under it stood an old man baking big pieces of pita bread—which we dipped into olive oil and covered with seeds. This was accompanied by delicious salads and refreshing tea.

As a parting gift, our guide presented me with a staff—a stout stick like that used by the original Moses.

If you've ever traveled to Israel, you are well aware that the airport security is extremely intense and thorough. Since the staff was too large to fit inside my suitcase, I carried it in my hand.

At security, a stern Israeli official barked, "Mister, what do you have there? And who gave it to you?" His tough demeanor was unnerving and gave me the feeling I had committed some federal offense.

I was flustered for a moment, thinking he was going to confiscate the item, so I responded, "Sir, all I know is, he told me his name was Moses."

Suddenly, this gruff man began to grin, "Go ahead," he smiled. "It's all right."

A Second Meeting

The following year I received a call that Sharon was going to be in Washington, D.C., and would like to meet with me again. On short notice, I flew to the nation's capital.

The following morning, one of our Fellowship leaders joined me for breakfast and drove me to meet the Prime Minister.

In our private, relaxed meeting, we touched on two matters—the prophetic future of Israel and a subject close to his heart, farming and agriculture. It was a topic we both knew well.

I still laugh about what happened earlier that morning. Vangie always makes sure I have my herbal vitamins with me whenever I travel, and prepares two daily packets—one to boost my energy and the other to relax and calm me. Well, I was so excited about meeting Sharon, I reached into the wrong pocket, and took the "relaxing" pills.

Fortunately, the effects didn't hit me until the meeting was over and I was riding in my host's car. He got me to the airport and the next thing I remember was waking up in Los Angeles!

"Passport! Passport!"

In our travels there have often been some unexpected surprises.

I will never forget what took place in the tiny village of Villars-sur-Ollon in the Swiss Alps. We were there as guests of Ara Tchividjian and his family—our longtime family friends with an Armenian heritage. He had left Turkey as a two-year-old with his mother and aunt because his father and grandfather were killed during the massacre.

One afternoon while Vangie was at the local beauty shop—the "coiffure"—I wandered around the shops.

The clerk at a men's store was very cordial. As I was leaving, I noticed that she quickly ran to the back and picked up the phone.

About two minutes later, as I was walking down a street, a tall, serious-looking special forces policeman was blocking my path. He was quickly joined by other officers.

"Passport! Passport!" they demanded in their broken English.

I tried to explain that my wife had my passport, but it was no use. They hurriedly hauled me off to the local jail and placed me in a cell.

I didn't know it, but at the time there was an international manhunt underway for one of the most notorious terrorists of the day, Carlos "The Jackal." He was actually Ramirez Sanchez, a Venezuelan, who was wanted for a series of bombings and murders of Western targets in Israel and Europe. Since the major oil ministers were meeting in nearby Geneva (and he had threatened them), there was a high alert in the area.

That day I was wearing aviator sun glasses and a Russian hat. With my dark complexion, the saleslady at the store thought I looked exactly like the picture she had seen in the papers of the notorious Carlos.

Finally, at my insistence, the police phoned Mr. Tchividjian, who explained that we were his guests. They drove me to his home for positive identification where we were served refreshments. There were no hard feelings. In fact, there was plenty to laugh about.

Carlos was eventually caught, convicted, and is now serving a life sentence in a French prison.

Danger Signs

In country after country, God has given us favor by

establishing relationships—and opening doors which continue to swing wider and wider.

Over the years we have been fortunate to make many journeys to Nigeria. The Fellowship is strong and flourishing in that nation and continues to have a major influence at many levels.

One particular trip was during a time when the U.S. government was warning people not to travel there unless absolutely necessary due to the corruption and violence. However, we did not alter our plans because (1) we believed God would protect us and (2) we knew the local Fellowship leaders would look out for our safety.

Usually, when we arrive in a foreign land, we know the person who is going to greet us. This trip was different. A woman whom we had never met before took charge. Even though she was not wearing a government uniform of any kind, whatever she told the baggage handlers or soldiers, they quickly rushed to oblige.

Seated at the customs desk was a man who had the evil-eye, ready to give us the third degree. Our greeter grabbed our passports, uttered a few words, and we breezed right past him.

When over-zealous young kids bombarded us, wanting to carry our luggage for money, she gave them one piercing look, pointed her finger, and they fled.

We soon learned that she was not only a member of the Fellowship, but a base commander in the Nigerian Army, holding a position of authority.

WHAT A CHANGE!

About two years later, we traveled through the same airport to attend one of our international conventions and were surprised at the complete change. People were friendly and courteous and handled themselves professionally.

This was primarily due to a change in government. In 1999, a man named Olusegun Obasanjo began an eight-year term as president of Nigeria.

We were honored to be invited to his private residence for breakfast. It was a California-style home with white marble floors.

Vangie and I were seated on each side of Obasanjo and others took their places down the long table. Before us sat several boxes of Kellogg's Rice Krispies.

There was a large picture window in the room and soon a baby giraffe and several other animals walked before our eyes. What a picturesque setting.

When it came time to order our meal, Obasanjo said, "I'll have Rice Krispies." I echoed, "I'll take the same as the President."

Before long, however, platter after platter of cooked breakfast dishes were placed on the table.

That afternoon, on a visit to his nearby office, he shared with me how he had been a general, but because he exposed corruption, was thrown into prison. "It was the best thing that ever happened to me, because it was there

I found Jesus."

After being freed, he ran for president and won. This was the first general in African history who held free elections and eventually turned the democratic government over to someone else.

I told him how impressed I was with the changes I saw in the country, starting with the airport. "No more bribes!" he proudly announced. "And we have prosecuted the road robbers who intimidated the police and stole from our citizens."

The president, being a Christian, had built a small chapel on the grounds. Quite a contrast from the former Muslim president who had erected a mosque.

Every Sunday morning there was always a service—and visiting dignitaries were extended an invitation. Seated next to me in the chapel was a Russian who was in the country working on an electric power project. We have attended this service many times over the years and have always felt the touch of God in this holy place.

While in power, Obasanjo personally taught a Sunday School class before the regular service.

"Just Tell Your Story"

On a later visit I asked him if he would honor us by being a featured speaker at an international convention of the Fellowship which was to be held in Abuja, the capital of Nigeria, built in the center of the nation. It is a modern city, unlike anything you would expect in this African nation.

Over 35,000 attended this event held at the National Stadium—guests flew in from Asia, Australia, Europe, the U.S. and Latin America.

On the night of his speech, as we were seated in a special box above the stage, he turned to me and asked, "What do you want me to say?"

"Just tell your story," I responded—"where you were, and how Christ found you and changed your life."

This was a diversified crowd that included average citizens, plus judges, bankers, and many high level government officials.

I will never forget his courageous message, with the capital city as a backdrop, as he expanded on the events of his life. "I am not sorry for the experience of being in prison. It turned out to be a blessing for me. I learned things I would have never known, but most important, someone came and gave me a Bible and told me about Jesus."

He explained, "At first I found the scriptures that told me how God would pour out wrath on His enemies. And I said, 'Lord, do that for me.'" Then he added, "But later I began to read the verses about love—and I realized that if I was going to receive God's love I had to demonstrate it! I had to forgive my enemies."

Finally, he told how he discovered a verse that read, "All power is in the hand of God." Day after day he sat in his cell imagining the hand of God at work in his own life—and soon he was released.

Our convention was moved by the life journey of this humble man, yet strong leader.

During our visit, Obasanjo, was so kind, treating us like royalty—showing his respect for the Fellowship.

A Bold Invitation

Prior to this convention, flying from England on a British aircraft, I suddenly became heavily burdened and started to weep. What wounded my heart was the fact that so many in Nigeria were still deeply entrenched in witchcraft and I longed to see them set free from this bondage.

During the conference, this was something I could not shake from my spirit—even though the attendees appeared as though they were far from such Satanic influence.

Nevertheless, on the final night of the convention, I poured out my heart and boldly made this statement at the end of my message: "If there is any witchcraft in your life, you can be set free right now by the power of the Almighty. You can communicate directly with God and no longer need to go through any medium or resort to voodoo or the occult."

Then I announced, "If you are ready to denounce witchcraft and be totally free, I want you to get out of your seat and run to the front."

I only said this once, and 5,000 men and women rushed to the front of the platform for prayer—some running on the track of the stadium for a quarter of a mile!

"Would You Pray for Me?"

Recently, we have been warmly received by the new President of Nigeria, "Goodluck" Jonathan—another outstanding Christian leader. We have enjoyed speaking at the morning prayer meeting he conducts regularly, after which he invited us to have breakfast with him at his residence.

On another trip to Africa, one particular day he took me by the hand and asked Vangie and his top aide to go with him into a private room. "Would you pray for me?" he asked.

What an honor! When I was about to pray, he rose from his chair and knelt down before me so I could lay my hands on his head and seek God on his behalf—and for Nigeria, the land he loved.

To read the headlines today, it would be easy to conclude that the world is in total disarray and falling apart, but I see things differently. There is an army of men and women rising up in every corner of the world who understand that God holds all power in heaven and on earth.

The Archbishop

The leaders of our Fellowship come from a wide variety of church backgrounds. For example, the president of our organization in Italy is Catholic, and during one of our conventions in Venice, he invited several priests from both the Catholic and Armenian Orthodox Church to be his guests.

At the banquet, Vangie and I became acquainted with Archbishop Luigi Accogli from the Vatican. He was an international diplomat of the Catholic Church.

During our conversation, he told us why he accepted the invitation to drive all the way from Rome. "I was thinking to myself, why would I go to be with businessmen? So I prayed about it and the Holy Spirit gave me these exact words, 'Because I am in the midst of those people.'"

The Archbishop became a wonderful friend, inviting us to visit the Vatican where we met with Pope John Paul II. I sensed that he had a strong aura of faith and I was deeply impressed.

I give glory to God when I realize how barriers of culture, language, race, and religion are being torn down.

"You've Got to See This"

Journey with us to the Congo! It's very name speaks of danger—a country of 71 million that has known unprecedented violence and bloodshed.

Vangie and I have made several visits to this West African nation, but on a recent trip we realized that despite, the conflicts that have gripped this area, there is an amazing spiritual fabric that is providing strength to the people.

Today, the Fellowship has hundreds of chapters in every corner of this country—and has been heralded by both government and civilian leaders as a strong moral force in this war-torn land.

One of our first trips here was in 1995, to speak at an international convention of the Fellowship in the capital city of Kinshasa. At the time, the country was called Zaire, and the legendary dictator, Mobutu, was the president.

He had been in power several years and people are often surprised to learn that Mobutu personally gave permission for the Fellowship to operate in his country. Many of the leaders of our organization held strategic positions in business, education, and government.

I'll never forget looking out from the convention platform. Before me were 8,000 Congolese men and women packed into the large building. When the service began, they were swaying back and forth, singing unto the Lord. It was such a beautiful sight that I motioned for Vangie to come to the platform. "You've got to see this," I whispered.

THE DICTATOR

When the convention ended, the Fellowship leaders were excited to tell us, "President Mobutu would like to meet you and we have arranged all the details."

The next day we were escorted onto a luxury government-owned French Falcon executive aircraft, jetting our way to a small village where Mobutu was raised and had a large residential compound. Joining us were some of our Fellowship leaders who also held positions in government.

The home was impressive, with flamingos roaming on the grounds.

We were told this would be a short visit, but Mobutu was familiar with the Fellowship and our talk went on at length. "Could you stay for a barbecue with my family?" he asked. We were delighted to accept his kind invitation.

As you may have gathered, I am a firm believer in prayer and take every opportunity to bring people, regardless of their position in life, to a closer relationship with God. At the conclusion of the day, I said, "Mr. President, I would like to pray for you."

Mobutu bowed his head and I laid my hands on his shoulders and began to pray. This autocratic leader seemed genuinely moved.

Some time later, back in the U.S., I met a man who was a close friend of the Mobutu family. When I shared our visit, he exclaimed, "You put your hand on him? You are lucky to be alive. Nobody touches Mobutu!"

I wish I could tell you that this encounter caused the dictator to look into his heart and change his ways, but it was not the case. However, I am thankful that God used him in allowing the Fellowship to operate freely and thrive during his years in power.

CROWDS AT THE AIRSTRIP

It has been amazing to see the hand of God at work in this nation, despite its many problems. The Fellowship has brought a message of hope to so many cities and villages.

On one visit, we were invited to speak in the city of Goma, and to make a side trip "safari" to Virunga, a national animal reserve. Evidently, word spread regarding our schedule. When the small commercial plane landed at an airstrip on the way, both sides of the runway were filled with people dressed in their finest, singing and excitedly waving at our plane.

"What's all this?" I wanted to know.

"They heard you were coming today and wanted to greet you. These people are members of our chapters in this area," our host explained to us. Even the local governor was on hand. Overwhelmed by their expressions of goodwill, we extended our thanks to everyone we could.

As we drove to our final destination, in village after village, men, women, and children lined the streets to welcome us. Many of the men wore ties and jackets. Their genuine enthusiasm deeply touched our hearts and we stopped the car time after time to shake their hands. They wanted to honor us because we represented an organization which was forever changing lives and we were humbled at their response.

During our travels in the Congo, we came across a fishing village that did not have a chapter of the Fellowship. We were preparing to have a lunch of fresh fish right from the lake. We looked around, wondering where International Vice President, John Carrette, was. When we found him, he was sharing Christ with a group of young fishermen nearby.

He was telling them about the organization and praying with each one. Instantly, a new chapter was formed!

John Carrette has faithfully served the Fellowship in his position for many years. His great love is to help people discover how real Christ can be to them through a relationship with the Holy Spirit.

A Deadly Conflict

Mobutu became a controversial figure on the international scene, primarily because of brutality and corruption. He was accused of syphoning billions of dollars from the struggling economy for his personal use. The dictator insisted that his photo be prominently displayed everywhere and demanded to be called "Father of the Nation." Government employees were required to wear lapel pins with an engraving of his likeness.

With Zaire literally falling apart at the seams, rebel forces, aided by support from the neighboring governments of Rwanda, Burundi, and Uganda, were able to drive Mobutu into exile. He fled in 1997 and died in Morocco shortly thereafter of prostate cancer.

Rising to leadership was Laurent-Desire Kabila, who installed a new constitution and renamed the country, The Democratic Republic of Congo (DRC). Sadly, however, the bloodshed continued. During the next several years, more than 5 million perished—either from gunshots, torture, or because of famine and disease that spread through the displaced population. There was also widespread sexual violence.

This hostility has been called the most deadly conflict since World War II.

In 2001, President Kabila was assassinated by one of his own bodyguards, and was succeeded by his son, Joseph (who is very much aware of the work of our organization). Today, many of the new cabinet members are in our Fellowship.

SPEAKING TO THE NATION

On our most recent visit to the Congo, our director there, an eye surgeon, took me to visit officials at several government offices. I noticed that the top judge of the military was wearing a Fellowship lapel pin.

Later, we met the Attorney General, who told me, "I used to be head of your chapters in the Goma area. I would not be in this position today without the training I received in the Fellowship, learning how to communicate and work with people."

Media reporters dogged our footsteps. When I was introduced to the president of the Senate, the dignified man told me, "I've been watching you on television and you're a very popular man." Then he joked, "I'd better watch out. If you ran for an office here, you'd probably be elected!"

On a serious note, he added. "I want you to know that your organization has an extremely good reputation in our nation."

One high-ranking senator, who was a strong Christian, arranged for me to speak the next Sunday morning at the National Cathedral. Most important, the message God gave me was televised to the entire nation.

Danny's Turn-Around

I cannot begin to explain the love we feel for the people of West Africa. The leaders of the Fellowship have a passion to see lives changed, which is why our chapters are growing and are so effective.

A major convention for French-speaking African nations was recently held in Ouagadougou, Burkina Faso (formerly Upper Volta). Hundreds of delegates flew in from many countries with stirring reports of what God was doing in their homelands.

To show their hospitality, each nation brought Vangie and me special gifts. I was presented with a vibrant, colorful cape, and also a king's robe. To show my appreciation, I put them on right there and then. The people cheered and cheered—a moment I will never forget.

Far more important, however, was their response to the messages given during this conference. They left with a renewed commitment to see their nations spiritually transformed.

From there we flew to Accra, Ghana, to meet with more of our leaders. It is also the home of Danny Mawuenyega, the International Secretary of the Fellowship.

Danny is a business and agricultural leader in Ghana, with strong connections in the government. Among other enterprises, his farms export millions of pineapples each year.

This is quite a leap forward from the problems he faced in the past. Many years ago, Danny's business ventures were in financial difficulty. He owed money to practically every bank in town, but then he heard about a meeting of Christian businessmen.

The reason he decided to attend was because there would be a free lunch—which sounded good at the time.

On his arrival, however, he was in for a big shock. As he tells it, "I looked around the room and saw many of the bankers I owed money to." So he quietly found a place in the back of the room to remain inconspicuous.

The speaker that day related the story of his wayward past and how all of his dreams had come crashing down before he turned his life over to the Lord. Then the man said, "If you are here and want to make a fresh start, I would like you to come to the front so I can pray with you."

"That's me," Danny said to himself. Yet, because of the bankers present, he felt embarrassed and stayed in his seat.

However, the convicting power of God's Spirit was so strong that Danny finally walked to the front. "It was the greatest decision I ever made," he told me.

From that moment forward, his life—and his economic future—experienced a dramatic turn-around.

Today he is a valued officer of our international organization.

The King

At a recent luncheon of our board members in Accra, my longtime friend, Senator Fred Brume from Nigeria walked in —bringing with him a distinguished-looking gentleman dressed in an ornate gown. We found out he was a king of one of the most important regions of Ghana who had been a close friend of the Senator since university days. They had served on the World Bank together.

During lunch, I asked if I could trade seats with Danny, who was seated next to the king. This was more than providential. During our conversation, I began sharing with him about the Lord—and a few minutes later he expressed his need to give his life to Christ.

Right there, in the hotel, the king prayed to receive Jesus as his Savior.

It was a memorable day.

Austrian President Kurt Waldheim and his wife, Madame Elizabeth with Richard and Vangie

Prime Minister
Ariel Sharon in Israel

Ara Tchividjian (left)
with police and
Richard in
Switzerland

Nigerian Presidents Olusegun Obasanjo (left)
and Goodluck Johathan (right)

Partial crowd of 35,000 at Nigerian stadium

Archbishop Luigi Accogli and Richard at the Vatican Gardens in Rome

With Pope John Paul II

Longtime friend Lee Iacocca, American business icon. Served as president of Ford Motors and as chairman of the Chrysler Corporation

Philippine President Fidel V. Ramos

Chapter 11

Flags of Faith

In the first chapter of this book, I shared the amazing impact of the Fellowship on the nation of Nicaragua. Let me tell you how this is continuing with even greater intensity.

As our work began to mushroom in that country, during a meeting with Daniel Ortega, he told me, "We have our elections soon and I would like you to come to the convention of the Sandinistas and open it in prayer."

I was shocked. After all, I was an American capitalist and he was a Marxist socialist.

"What would you like me to pray for?" I inquired.

"Just the same things you have prayed for me," he replied. So I agreed.

On the opening day of the convention, about 1,000 jammed the auditorium. It was quite a sight, with flags and banners all over the place. I was sitting on the second row, directly behind Ortega. On both sides of him were overstuffed chairs with delegates seated from Cuba, Russia, and Venezuela.

After a short video extolling Ortega, the announcer said, "Now we are going to have a prayer by Dr. Shakarian."

The moment he spoke those words, everyone in the auditorium immediately stood to their feet at attention and bowed their heads. They were very respectful.

I began, "Before I pray, let me ask how many of you have been to one of our meetings?" Half the people raised their hands.

My prayer was that the Spirit of God would rest on each of them personally and that they would know the ways of Christ.

Some may question how I could pray for those with such a different political persuasion. I can only point to Saul in the New Testament. Christ came to this man in a vision, despite his terrible reputation. He was totally transformed and became Paul the Apostle—a champion of Christianity.

We never go into a country with the intention to change the political system but to change the hearts of the people—which perhaps is why we are so accepted. We welcome everyone, just as they are.

Remember, our leaders come from the business world, not from the pulpit. If I had been a preacher, I doubt I would have been invited to such a convention.

I am happy to report that countless Sandinista have joined our Fellowship.

What Happened to the Bull?

One day I was conversing with a group of Sandinista military leaders and remembered something from the dim past. Several decades earlier, my father had sent a prize bull to Central America to help raise the milk production of dairies through artificial insemination.

There was a short man standing before me—a tough military officer who had made life and death decisions over so many people. Something inside led me to ask, "Are you the man my dad gave the bull to?"

"Yes, I am," he answered. "I knew your father."

Next to him was a tall, rough-looking man with a knife scar down one cheek. He replied in a deep voice, "Yeah, I knew your dad, too. We liked your father. He had a great sense of humor."

I looked up at him and said, "Wonderful! But what happened to the bull? Did you use it for its intended purpose?"

"Oh, yes. But then we decided we would eat the capitalist bull!" And they all started to laugh.

"Well," I responded, "The joke's on you, because my father anointed that bull with holy oil and prayed for it before sending it here. So that anointing is now inside of you!" They laughed again—but I'm sure it made them think.

Each of those men have now attended one of our Fellowship chapter meetings.

A New Life for Luis

A frequent stop for me in Nicaragua is to appear on evening television shows. One was hosted by Luis Manual Mora Sanchez. He is who you would call the Bill O'Reilly of local TV. He never hesitated to call out the conservatives or the Sandinistas if he was alerted to or saw any form of corruption.

There had been many attempts on his life—and the bullet holes in his car are proof!

An attorney friend had asked Luis numerous times to join him at a luncheon for businessmen. Finally, he agreed and was brought to a meeting of our Fellowship.

As he listened to the stories of men who had experienced a dramatic change, he thought of his own chaotic life. Women, tangled relationships, and suffering from deep depression.

He listened intently and thought to himself, "I am spiritually dead inside." Because of what he heard that day, he decided to follow Christ.

Soon after, he attended one of our seminars, which included people from many political persuasions.

In the middle of the meeting, a man came up to him and asked, "Are you Luis Mora?"

"Yes, I am," he answered.

"Let's go outside."

The man told him, "I am the brother of the person who killed the TV newsman from your station two weeks ago. We were very angry with you. You said terrible things about our leader, Daniel Ortega. You even insulted his wife, and I wanted to kill you."

Luis is rather short in stature, and thought he was about to be in for the fight of his life. He began looking around for a chair or anything of substance to defend himself.

The man kept talking. "Yes, I wanted to kill you, but I came to God through this Fellowship. I forgive you in the name of Jesus. And I ask you to forgive me for what my brother did to your newsman."

Luis was quite shaken, but very relieved. However, no sooner had he taken his seat in the meeting when another man called him outside. He introduced himself as a Sandinista mayor from a nearby city. "You don't know how much I hated you, but now I have found a new way of life through the Fellowship. Will you forgive me?"

Amazed, Luis Mora knew he had made the right decision and became a new man in Christ. He told me, "People who wanted to kill me are now my friends. They are guests in my home and eat at my table. I have a peace I never knew."

During each interview on his television program he gave me the entire hour to answer call-in questions and pray for the people.

What an undeniable transformation in the life of Luis!

FINDING A PURPOSE

During a press conference in Managua, a French journalist raised his hand and asked a penetrating question. Normally I would have answered immediately, yet felt led to respond, "I will answer it later, but will you come and sit next to me?" He did.

When the press conference was over, I began talking with him about the purpose of his life. As we were conversing, I suddenly felt something on the back of my neck. It was his arm!

The next thing I knew, he put his head on my chest and started weeping as he invited the Lord into his heart.

That day, as I looked around the room, over a period of several years I had the privilege of leading nearly every one of those television and newspaper reporters to Christ.

Today, over one half of the entire population of Nicaragua has personally prayed with a member of our Fellowship.

Curious Reporters

Before Ortega was re-elected as President of Nicaragua, I took the bold step of inviting him to speak at a world convention we were having in Miami.

He responded, "Richard, as a former Head of State, I need to have a diplomatic invitation." He had been quite angry with America because of the way he felt he had recently been treated.

The State Department refused to sign off on a visit, so he sent his wife to represent him. This proved to be a disaster. The hotel would not allow her to stay there since there were Nicaraguan workers who wanted to kill her because of what their families had suffered under her husband's rule. We arranged for her to be a guest at another hotel several miles away.

The international news media, including Telemundo, caught wind of the story and there were Latin American reporters and satellite dishes waiting at the convention hotel. "Mr. Shakarian, how could you invite such a man to this convention? Don't you know what he has done?"

My response was, "We believe that every person, regardless of their past, should have the opportunity to ask God to forgive them." The message of forgiveness and a better life was being broadcast by the secular media daily throughout the world.

The reporters were so curious they attended our meetings and listened to men whose lives had experienced a dramatic turn-around. One of the stories became a front page feature in the Sunday edition of the *Miami Herald*.

Ortega did appear at our convention, but only via a video he had prepared. There was no hint of politics, rather a message of God's forgiveness.

If you have followed the events of Nicaragua during his last political campaign, Ortega not only renounced terrorism, but displayed an American flag on his stage. That was quite a reversal!

THE RED FLAG

In the nation of Honduras, plans were made for 5,000 meetings in schools, businesses, and other locations during a 10 day period. The goal was to pray for one person in each family.

However, flying into the country, I realized that even that number of meetings could not reach the entire nation. Then the Lord gave me divine inspiration. I thought about the story of Joshua and Rahab, the woman in Jericho who hid the two Israeli spies, then hung a red cord from her window as a signal to Joshua's armies that her house was to be spared (Joshua 2).

On my arrival, I went to a store and purchased a piece of red cloth—it was my red flag of faith.

During my many television interviews, I draped it over my legs. When the reporters asked about the flag, I explained that it represented the healing and forgiving red blood of Christ flying over the nation.

Then, speaking before the national congress, I draped the red cloth over the podium and stated, "Today, this red flag does not stand for the Partido Nacional de Honduras (conservatives) or the Partido Liberal de Honduras (liberals). This flag represents the blood of Jesus over Honduras."

The entire congress rose to their feet and began to applaud.

After the session, many in the congress, including a former President, approached me, wanting to let me know, "I belong to the Fellowship."

After this impressive event, I spoke to the combined Joint Chiefs of Staff, the equivalent of our Pentagon. Then to the Military Academy, to address over 2,000 of the nation's future leaders.

During that 10 day period, more than 350,000 individuals were prayed with personally by one of our volunteers.

The stories we heard that week were unforgettable and awesome.

One of our teams conducted a meeting at a university,

and at the conclusion a student came up to the leader and showed him a note she had written to her parents. It read, "Dear Momma and Pappa. I love you. Please forgive me for what I am going to do, but I have no hope. Your loving daughter."

She and her boyfriend had made a suicide pact for that very day.

With a smile creased on her lips, she told the leader, "I don't need this letter anymore. Now I have hope."

From the Poorest to the Richest

At the conclusion of our outreach in Honduras, I was driven down to the Navy base to speak to the cadets and officers, after which, they took me out on a Navy gunboat.

On the way back to the hotel, a man who was not a member of the Fellowship, but had been with us that day, asked, "Would you please come to my small restaurant to eat?"

It was a very modest place. After the meal, one of our team members whispered to me, "This man wants to give his life to the Lord"—and, of course, we were thrilled to pray with him.

In a moment, out walked his wife, his son, and four humble kitchen workers. What a joy to lead this entire group to the Lord.

We were leaving the restaurant at midnight when one of our Fellowship members, Oswaldo Quiroz, begged me, "Richard, please come with me to pray for one of the wealthiest men in Honduras who is dying of cancer."

Being totally exhausted, I hesitated, but he insisted, "Richard, you just have to; he is a business partner." Oswaldo himself is a successful entrepreneur.

The family was from Lebanon and were Arabs. Of course, as is their custom, they served us tea. After visiting with the sons for about an hour, we went to the man's bedroom and prayed for him.

As we were about to leave the home, the sons opened their hearts to receive the Lord.

It was exactly 2:00 A.M. as the three of them stood on the curb outside their mansion and committed their lives to Christ. I looked up at the star-filled sky and said to the Lord, "Thank You for the great privilege You have given to me. In the length of three hours I have seen Your grace extended from the poorest people in the nation to the richest. Your love and forgiveness is truly for every person."

LILLIAN'S TEARS

In September 2011, I was back in Honduras.

The very first morning, after arriving in San Pedro Sula, I was told that a reporter from the *La Prensa* newspaper was there to interview me regarding the Fire Team outreach which was underway.

Lillian, the journalist, was very professional. She asked all the right questions, but after about 20 minutes I began to rapidly tell her one story after another of desperate people who had found new hope—an alcoholic who had been set free, a son who forgave his abusive father, a husband who began to love his wife and family again. Following several of these accounts, she looked at me and asked, "Mr. Shakarian, is this true? Can someone really be changed in just one meeting?"

I responded, "No, absolutely not. But when God touches you, you will be changed in an instant!"

She seemed to be shaken by the answer. Then her hands went up to her face as she bowed her head. To my surprise, I noticed tears falling down her cheeks and dropping onto the table.

Through the interpreter I asked, "Lillian, would you like to accept the Lord for yourself?" In a moment we were praying, and when she lifted her head, her face was shining like a star.

She told me, "Mr. Shakarian, I have been a reporter for six years. I didn't realize until yesterday how much this job had hardened me. I was assigned to report on the death of a young boy who had been murdered. It was a very emotional case, but I personally felt nothing. Even when his heartbroken father told me about his son—I just felt numb and empty."

She continued, "But, when you were telling me the stories of renewed lives I sensed something stirring on the inside—I began to feel human again." After our prayer, she exclaimed, "Now I am so happy."

Our U.S.A. Vice President, Joe Ortega, and his wife Rosa, arrived a few minutes later. Excited about what had just happened, I showed them a picture of the reporter. They exclaimed, "Oh, we just saw her outside. She was waiting for her car, but the expression on her face looked like she was soaring above the clouds."

That week, our 2,000 volunteers reached 695,000 people in 21,000 locations.

Today, we have several hundred chapters of men and women in Honduras. They have personally prayed with more that 40 percent of the population.

I must admit that when I received the word from the Lord that we were to pray for one person in every family in a nation, I did not think it was humanly possible. I have been amazed to see the promise of God coming true in country after country.

I write this with deep gratitude to the thousands of individuals who have joined us in this vision.

Addressing Honduran Congress

Chapter 12

Truly, a Better Life

A few days ago, Vangie and I were reflecting on the rewarding life God has given us. I told her, "While it is wonderful to travel the globe and see such marvelous things taking place in the Fellowship, there is no place like home."

A Christmas Tradition

I especially look forward to Christmas. This is when the entire family gets together and enjoys the many traditions that have been handed down through the generations.

Dinner always includes turkey, plus an Armenian pilaf with raisins, dates, and slivered almonds. Add the Christmas salad and countless side dishes including marinated string beans with onions and tomatoes—we hardly have room for the pies!

After the meal, each person is handed a bell or something to ring while we gather around the piano and sing Christmas songs. Then it's time for me to sit down and tell the story of the birth of Jesus. I never read it from a book, but simply share it from my heart. When my father was alive, he was the one who always told the Christmas Story, and it is my joy to continue this tradition.

Opening the presents comes last. It is a very happy family time.

Proud Parents

As I mentioned earlier we have been blessed with four beautiful daughters. While each have talents in their own right, Vangie and I are most proud of their personal relationship with the Lord.

Our oldest is Denice, who always has a smile on her face, even since she was a baby. Following her studies at Oral Roberts University, she married H. B. "Toby" Halicki, who wrote, produced, and directed the movie, "Gone in 60 Seconds." It became an instant classic because of its unforgettable car chase scenes.

Then, in 1989 he began shooting "Gone in 60 Seconds 2" in which both he and his new bride, Denice, would star.

During the production, as Toby prepared to shoot one of the most dramatic stunt sequences, the unthinkable occurred when a 160-foot water tower rigged to fall later in the scene collapsed prematurely. The tower snapped a supporting cable which sheared a nearby power pole. It came crashing to the ground, instantly killing Toby as crowds of fans, the press, and Denice looked on in horror. Denice was a bride and widow in the same summer. Only her faith in the Lord got her through this difficult time.

Ten years later, Denice was the executive producer of the remake of her husband's original "Gone in 60 Seconds." It starred Nicholas Cage, Angelina Jolie, and Robert Duvall, becoming an international blockbuster. She was engaged to the late Robert Kardashian.

Our second child, Cynthia, was born with a congenital heart condition. When she was just four months old, we were told by a pediatric cardiologist, "She will need surgery before she starts school." When I placed my ear to her tiny chest, the sound of her heartbeat mimicked that of a train.

At nine months, a panel of doctors at White Memorial Hospital in Los Angeles gathered around Cynthia in a large circle, examining and discussing her case. They all concluded that heart surgery would be in her future.

I cannot calculate how many prayers were sent heavenward on Cynthia's behalf—including Oral Roberts laying hands on her. Before entering kindergarten, the doctors examined her one more time—and our prayers were answered. They found no problem! She has lived a healthy, normal life.

As a child, we always loved her long, thick, Armenian hair. She has a wonderful sense of humor.

Cynthia has great tenacity, which enabled her to be extremely successful in her real estate career. She entered business at the age of 18 and was the number one producer in her office for years—and has a room full of trophies.

Brenda was the next addition to our family and at a very early age displayed her creative flair. We first noticed this when she began sketching drawings of beautiful gowns and dresses. After attending ORU, she went on to start her own business as a fashion designer. Her line of clothes was called the "Shakarian Collection" and was featured at high-end boutiques. The Las Vegas Hilton said her collection was the fastest selling line they ever carried.

Brenda always had a heart to help people so she began

a foundation for children called "Love in Action," working in several nations helping kids with medicine, books, education, and sports. She also organized large community events.

She is a gifted speaker helping to start our first International Women's and Youth Conferences. She is currently Executive of International Relations and Media for the Fellowship. She created our new television series, titled *No Borders*, featuring real life turn-around stories.

Her husband, Terence Rose, is involved in international finance.

Our "baby" is Suzanne, who brought much sunshine into our home. To this day we laugh about what happened in first grade. Her teacher asked, "Suzanne, what nationality are you?" She replied, "I am Armenian and something else—but I don't know what."

Once she arrived home, she asked her mom the same question, to which Vangie told her, "You're half Norwegian." Vangie doubted the teacher would believe her since Suzanne looks so Armenian. Vangie joked, "You probably have Norwegian in your big toe!"

Suzanne is blessed with a tender heart, which she displays by her thoughtfulness to others. She loves to entertain and is the one who plans our family functions.

All of our girls have been industrious and shine in different areas. Suzanne has a stellar reputation as a makeup artist and works with weddings, special events, and some of the leading department stores in Southern California. Her husband, Patrick St. Peter, is a CPA and financial consultant.

When our daughters all get together, you can guarantee there will be plenty of fun and laughter.

Now a new generation is emerging. As I write this, Cynthia's daughter, Rachel Evangeline, has graduated from Southern Methodist University and is in Law School at Pepperdine University in Malibu, with special studies at their branch campus in London. As a high achiever, she has an air of confidence and always strives to be the best at whatever she does, never allowing an obstacle to block her path. She is well loved and respected. People are drawn to her not only for her talents, but also for her sweet personality.

Brenda's two children, Blakeland Richard and Brianna Elizabeth, have been gifted with many talents. Brianna has had a tender heart for God since she was a little girl. She would tell kids about her faith on the playground.

Once, while we were dining in a restaurant, little Brianna wandered off to a nearby table. There we found her talking to complete strangers about the Lord.

She has a beautiful voice and sings at our events in different countries with her brother Blakeland. She attended Oral Roberts University and is continuing advanced studies. Since she is a computer whiz, I often ask her to help me at the office.

Blakeland is a born leader and has always been a person of sterling character his peers look to for counsel. As a high school basketball player, the press gave him plenty of coverage. More important, however, was what his coach said in front of the team after his final season. "Blake is the guy I always call on at crunch time. He displays a cool confidence under pressure that can be attributed to his strong faith in God."

He is the International Youth leader of the Fellowship and is at university studying economics and global finance.

Our daughters and grandchildren all share one thing in common. They are outgoing, optimistic, and never meet a stranger.

Vangie and I have certainly had our share of life's challenges, but we have never wavered in our faith. Our family is following the same path—being reassured and knowing that regardless of the circumstances, somehow, some way, God will bring them through.

In our travels around the world, Vangie is always a positive inspiration. She leads the Ladies of the Fellowship, and it is growing.

At times when we are faced with seemingly impossible situations, she looks beyond the circumstance and inspires all of us with her belief and confidence that God, who has begun great things in our lives, will fulfill His good plan. Her gentle spirit and care for the people has resulted in the love of many all over the world.

A Seed to the Nations

Over the years, I have been asked many times, "Richard, why do you believe your family was spared when so many others suffered because of the massacre in Armenia?"

To me, the answer is clear. It is because my great-grandparents took seriously the prophecy from God, delivered by Efim Klubniki, an 11-year-old boy in Kara Kala. They came to America knowing the Lord had directed their steps. They also believed the final words of the prophecy, that "God would prosper them and make them a seed to the nations."

This has certainly proven to be true.

In my father's original vision, he did not see chapters of the Fellowship, he saw people. Today, that is still our focus.

At the time my dad told me, "Richard, break the mold," neither of us knew exactly what this meant. It was years later when God showed me that we were to break down the confining walls of our chapter meeting rooms and venture out into the world—praying for one person in each family.

STANDING FIRM

Today, I take seriously the task of choosing those who lead the Fellowship. This means finding men who not only possess a passion for souls, but who demonstrate their commitment every day. I look for individuals who are personally active and diligent in bringing others to Christ. These are people who place God's work ahead of their own—making Him first in every aspect of their being.

When a person truly has a vision, they soon discover it is the vision that has *them!*

I also believe that in an organization you must have the spirit of the person who received the original vision. The spirit of my father was constantly reaching out to everyone he met—lifting them into the presence of the Lord.

Let me give you an example. In our search for the International Treasurer of the Fellowship, I looked at the lives of many individuals across the globe. One person stood head and shoulders above the crowd: Gideon Esurua, from Nigeria.

Even though Gideon had come from a rough background, after receiving Christ, his life and family completely changed. He is a geologist, real estate developer, and an entrepreneur with businesses in several nations. In his travels I saw him opening many new chapters and encouraging business men to move forward in the Fellowship.

When I chose him to be our Treasurer, I was asked, "Why Gideon?" The answer is simple: "He has a heart filled with compassion for others, is steadfast, and never wavers under pressure. He has total confidence in the Lord."

Gideon has proved to be an outstanding officer and a tremendous help to our organization.

A Childhood Lesson

I am always on the lookout for those whose faith is so unshakable they will stand firm in the face of any opposition. This is a lesson I learned as an eight-year-old boy.

One summer I was playing with two of my buddies in the dried-out San Gabriel riverbed behind our dairy farm. Before long, some older boys in their teens showed up and started to threaten us: "You can't play here. This is our river. Get out!"

We held our ground and didn't budge. After all, this was our place to play. But their next words really grabbed our attention. They jeered, "If you don't leave we are going to turn the bulls loose on you."

That did it! We scrambled out of there as fast as our legs could carry us.

It was the first and last time I ever ran from intimidation.

Today, I tell our leaders, "One day, someone is going to threaten to turn the bulls loose. And only you can decide whether you will stand firm in your faith or run."

From Belgium to Bali

Every day, we receive wonderful, positive reports from

our outstanding leaders around the world who tirelessly give of their time and resources. Space does not permit me to report everything that is taking place.

Across Africa, Europe, Russia, Central and South America, the Fellowship is spreading like a blazing fire. In the United States, where the work first began, new chapters are springing up from coast to coast.

Vangie and I recently returned from mainland China. New hope is being birthed everywhere in Asia and our dedicated leaders are praying and believing that millions of people will find a better life through Christ.

I am thrilled to report that Indonesia has hundreds of thriving chapters. This is one of the reasons our 2012 international convention was held in Bali.

The Fellowship today includes:

- Chapters in 148 nations
- 70 International Directors
- 21 Regional Vice-Presidents
- 148 National Presidents
- 608 National Officers
- 1,756 National Directors
- 8,000 Chapters
- 32,000 Chapter Officers

Each year, millions of people attend our events. It is also estimated that the time donated by our members annually is over 4.2 million hours. Tens of thousands of leaders are finding principles that dramatically improve their personal, business, and spiritual life.

As the largest Christian business organization in the world, the Fellowship works tirelessly to accomplish God's work of changing lives through meetings, conferences, outreach programs, television, short wave radio, the Internet, and other means.

LIKE A MIGHTY TREE

Today, the Fellowship is standing globally like a tall and mighty tree. Its roots are grounded and buried deep in the Spirit of God and the vision given to my father, Demos Shakarian.

Our International Headquarters in California represents the trunk of the tree—or the central hub of worldwide activity.

The branches are the thousands of chapters in nearly 150 nations. These have become a tremendous training ground for organizational and relational skills for business, religion, life, and family.

Only God knows how many millions are being encouraged and inspired through our chapters.

The sun never sets on this work and ministry, and through the Fellowship you can literally connect to the entire world. We are linking arms together in a common expression of our joy.

This movement is led by thousands of dedicated men and women who are united as one—regardless of culture or location. Our mission is to reach one person in every family in every nation—from presidents and prime ministers to ordinary men and women who are hungry and searching for a new beginning.

We are awakening individuals to the fact that there is more to life than living just for self. Each person has a God-given responsibility to impact the next generation.

It's Just the Beginning

At this very moment, somewhere on this planet called earth, a businessman is standing before a chapter meeting, opening his heart and telling his personal story of receiving a better life when he accepted Christ. It's even more exhilarating to realize that this is being duplicated thousands of times every week.

The reason we continue to be the happiest people is because we see despair turning to hope and broken hearts being filled with everlasting joy.

This is not the end of the story. We have already reached over 2 billion lives, and we are just beginning.

Will you join us in this heaven-ordained work that is transforming nations?

Vangie (center) with our daughters (left to right)
Cynthia, Brenda, Suzanne, and Denice

Our grandchildren, Blakeland Richard,
Rachel Evangeline, and Brianna Elizabeth

Blakeland receiving his
FGMBFI membership pin

FGBMFI 50th Anniversary Celebration

Fellowship Leaders — Planning to reach a continent

TO CONTACT THE AUTHOR OR TO
SCHEDULE HIM FOR SPEAKING ENGAGEMENTS:

RICHARD SHAKARIAN
P.O. BOX 19714
IRVINE, CA 92623

EMAIL: info.fgbmfi@gmail.com
INTERNET: www.fgbmfi.org
www.globalvisionbooks.com